Waiting for José

Waiting for José

THE MINUTEMEN'S PURSUIT OF AMERICA

HAREL SHAPIRA

WITH A NEW AFTERWORD BY THE AUTHOR

PRINCETON UNIVERSITY PRESS
PRINCETON AND OXFORD

Third printing, and first paperback printing,
with a new afterword by the author, 2018

Paperback ISBN 978-0-691-17844-8
Cloth ISBN 978-0-691-15215-8

Library of Congress Control Number: 2017940683

Title page photo (detail): Arizona National Guard Monitors Mexican Border.
© John Moore / Getty Images News. Courtesy of Getty Images.

British Library Cataloging-in-Publication Data is available

This book has been composed in Minion Pro

Printed on acid-free paper. ∞

Printed in the United States of America

3 5 7 9 10 8 6 4

America I've given you all and now I'm nothing.

—Allen Ginsberg, "America"

Estragon: Didi?

Vladamir: Yes.

Estragon: I can't go on like this.

Vladamir: That's what you think.

Estragon: If we parted? It might be better for us.

Vladamir: We'll hang ourselves tomorrow. Unless Godot comes.

Estragon: And if he comes?

Vladamir: We'll be saved.

—Samuel Beckett, *Waiting for Godot*

Contents

||||||||||||||||||||||||||

The Minutemen Chain of Command
||||||||||||||||||||||||||||||||||||||||||

Rank: President
Name: Chris Simcox
Handle: None
Age: 47
Home state: Arizona (moved from
Los Angeles to Arizona at the
end of 2001)
Military service: None

Rank: Comms leader
Name: Warren
Handle: Poker
Age: 74
Home state: Arizona
Military service: Thirty years;
stationed in Middle East during
numerous conflicts
Division: Military Intelligence Corps

Rank: Scout; search and rescue
Name: Bruce
Handle: Legolas
Age: 43
Home state: Kansas
Military service: Twenty years;
served in Iraq (Desert Storm)
Division: Marine Corps

Rank: Line leader
Name: Grant
Handle: Blowfish
Age: 68
Home state: Arizona
Military service: Twenty-two years;
served in Vietnam
Division: United States Army
Special Forces (Green Beret)

Rank: Stands post
Name: Stanley
Handle: Mussels
Age: 68
Home state: New Hampshire
Military service: Twenty-one years;
served in Vietnam
Division: Air Force

Rank: Stands post
Name: Earl
Handle: Tennessee
Age: 44
Home state: Tennessee
Military service: Fifteen years;
served in Iraq (Desert Storm)
Division: Army

Rank: Stands post
Name: Wade
Handle: Eagle-2
Age: 71
Home state: Colorado
Military service: Twenty-seven years; served in Vietnam
Division: Army

Rank: Stands post
Name: Gordon
Handle: Dune
Age: 69
Home state: Ohio
Military service: None

Rank: Head of administration
Name: Susan (married to Warren)
Handle: None
Age: 73
Home state: Arizona
Military service: Twenty-four years; stationed in Middle East during numerous conflicts
Division: Administrative work for Military Intelligence Corps

Acknowledgments

||||||||||||||||||||||||||||||

A FEW DAYS AFTER ARRIVING at the University of Chicago as an over-whelmed seventeen-year-old, I walked into Saskia Sassen's office. Every day since then, and indeed for what has now been over a decade, first in Chicago, then in London, and now in New York, Saskia Sassen and Richard Sennett have been my home away from home, opening their arms and doors for me wherever and whenever. Thank you, Saskia, and thank you Richard.

The University of Chicago is a truly special place, with teachers who are there because they want to teach. I was fortunate enough to have many wonderful teachers at Chicago, but no one was better than the great Moishe Postone, an intellectual in the honest sense of the word.

I became a sociologist through the experience of reading Mitch Duneier's *Slim's Table* at the very South Side Chicago diner where the book takes place. I still get goose bumps thinking back to the excitement I felt while looking around the diner to see if I could spot the wonderful characters Mitch writes about. I cannot begin to express the honor it has been to have had Mitch's support while attempting to reproduce for others, if even slightly, the kind of excitement Mitch's book produced in me.

I learned how to think at the University of Chicago, but I matured into a researcher at Columbia University.

I learned field methods from Herb Gans, a pillar of the ethnographic community. Herb taught me two critical things that I carried with me every moment in southern Arizona: (1) don't treat fieldwork as being that different from everyday life, and (2) always find out who throws away the trash: those folks are important.

In an amazing bit of luck, the Columbia housing office placed me in an apartment in the same building as Claudio Lomnitz, a scholar whose great mind is only surpassed by his great heart.

Craig Calhoun is a champion of a scholar and person. He is a rarity: an academic whose primary satisfaction comes from providing opportunities for others and doing what he can to make them succeed. As I was finishing up my dissertation, Craig offered me the Cadillac of postdocs: a three-year fellowship at his Institute for Public Knowledge at New York University, a true community if there ever was one.

Karen Barkey supported me from start to finish. When others questioned the wisdom of my place at Columbia, Karen championed my cause and guided me with her remarkable wisdom and warmth.

Throughout this project I turned to Sudhir Venkatesh for inspiration and guidance, and he offered me both with unparalleled generosity. More than anyone else, Sudhir taught me the craft of ethnography and kept me from drowning in its often treacherous waters.

I am truly at a loss for words trying to express how grateful I am to Shamus Khan for his remarkable mentorship and dear friendship. He gave more than I can account for. Let me try this: if there are sections in this book that are good, it is because Shamus made them so. How lucky we all are that Shamus will undoubtedly inspire, guide, and nurture so many students in the years to come.

Nadia Abu El-Haj, Gil Anidjar, Peter Bearman, Yinon Cohen, Victoria de Grazia, David Grazian, Alondra Nelson, and Diane Vaughan are all extremely special scholars who shared their wisdom and time with me even though I was not officially one of "their" students.

I had the good fortune of moving to New York University just as I began writing this book. While at NYU, Eric Klinenberg, Jeff Manza, and Harvey Molotch provided much inspiration and insight and guided me through even the most discouraging moments of writing.

From start to finish, the Princeton University Press family has been exceptional. Ellen Foos, Ryan Mulligan, and Anita O'Brien gave a lot of their time and skill to improving this book. Eric Schwartz is the kind of editor people say no longer exists. He is caring, he is intelligent, he has good taste, and he gives you his time. Indeed, Eric treated this book as if it were his own. I hope he is proud of what we have produced together.

Dave Brotherton and Shehzad Nadeem reviewed this book with great care and provided terrific and thoughtful comments. David Lobenstine dedicated himself to helping me express my thoughts in a prose that is accessible and attractive.

I thank Anita Fore, Daniel Fridman, Colin Jerolmack, Jooyoung Lee, David Madden, Ashley Mears, Erin O'Connor, Anatoly Pinsky, Alix Rule, Tyson Smith, Iddo Tavory, Clement Thery, and Lucia Trimbur for their help and camaraderie.

Throughout my time in Arizona as well as in New York, Sahand Boorboor and Livia Paggi provided rare friendship and support.

The majority of photos in this book were taken by the talented Andrea Dylewski, who traveled to the border with me on numerous occasions and repeatedly showed me new ways of seeing what was going on in front of my eyes.

I thank the members of the Minutemen Civil Defense Corps for their generosity, interest, and trust, which did not always come easy but always came in larger amounts than I had anticipated. The Minutemen did not make many requests, but the one I heard most often, and the one that I have taken most to heart, is simple but important: that I be fair and honest. I hope the Minutemen who read this book will find that I have fulfilled this request.

Minou Arjomand read and edited and enchanted every page of this book and continues to enchant every moment of my life. Thank you, Love.

Lastly, to my family: I thank my brother for his unwavering support and for making growing up a shared experience. And to my mother and father, quite simply, I thank you and love you for it all.

While I was doing research for this book, my grandfather Yaakov Shapira passed away. Yaakov was an amazing storyteller, and he had much to tell. For nearly a decade he survived the Second World War through a combination of guile, determination, and luck, which saw him enlist as a teenager in the Soviet Army, hitchhike to Tashkent where he exchanged sacks of flour for sacks of rice, and spend month after month evading capture in nooks and crannies. Even though the stories were not always pleasant, some of my fondest memories of growing up involve lying down on the cool concrete floor of my grandparents' steamy Haifa apartment and listening to him to speak. I dedicate this book to his memory.

KARL HOFFMAN

Preface: A Place on the Border

||||||||||||||||||||||||||||||||||||||

SITUATED AT THE CENTER OF THE SOUTHERN ARIZONA desert, the Valley[1] starts at the point where Mexico ends and the United States begins. In the Valley you can see as far as the eye will let you, its repetitive flatness spreading out in every direction until it hits the mountains that encase it. The terrain is composed of rough desert, with few roads but lots of mesquite trees, sagebrush, and cacti. Every now and then a patch of green breaks the overwhelming yellow. Anything man-made sticks out like a sore thumb; this is nature's place.

On summer days temperatures regularly reach triple digits. You can see waves of heat in the air; the landscape appears to undulate. In the winter monsoons flood the area, making the Valley's few roads impassible. The different seasons are known as much for the different species of wildlife they bring as they are for the change in weather. In the summer the hissing of rattlesnakes echoes; in the spring hundreds of tarantulas come out of hibernation.

At night the panoramic views shift from the earth to the skies. The nighttime darkness is so overwhelming that you can't see what's right in front of you, but above you can see more stars, with more crispness, than you ever thought possible. Locals joke about not having enough wishes for even a night's worth of shooting stars. But in the Valley's many vistas, what can be seen most clearly is the impact the border has had on life in America.

It's an impact we rarely hear about or take notice of, an impact whose influence is felt not just by immigrants, not just by those wishing to come to America, but by those already inside. It is an impact whose effects are best captured not through the sociological themes of culture and assimilation, or by turning toward economic indicators, but through the looming presence of walls and watchtowers, through taking a trip to the grocery store in the next town over and having to turn around because your pickup truck is too wide to pass the checkpoint that you must now go through.

Although the border is being fashioned by policy makers in Washington, D.C., determined by national interests and concerns and affecting the national economy, it is materializing, not simply as a symbol but as a concrete slab, at the local level. It is in places such as the Valley that the border transforms from an abstract idea about immigration and national security into walls, checkpoints, and Border Patrol agents, remaking the physical geography of places and the social geography of their inhabitants.

Apart from improvements local cattle ranchers have made on their land, until recently very little was built in the Valley. Most of the infrastructure in the area was created as a consequence of the mining boom, which hit the region in the nineteenth century and was sponsored by federal funds earmarked to support the mines. By extracting gold and silver, and later copper, mining companies thrived for the first half of the twentieth century and were the backbone of southern Arizona's economy. But by the 1950s many of the mines were depleted, and those that were not began to lose their purpose during the second half of the twentieth century when manufacturing in the United States began to decline.

Ranching, southern Arizona's other major industry, has suffered a similar fate. During the second half of the twentieth century, Arizona's land increasingly became valued not for its capacity to support agriculture but for its capacity to support residential and commercial development. Arizona's economy, once rooted in the rural, has been steadily urbanizing. Public lands, once set aside for grazing, have increasingly been sold off to developers. The resulting uncertainty associated with the tenure of public-grazing permits and decreasing economic returns has made ranchers a dying breed. The younger generations, meant to be inheritors of family ranches, have made the move toward the city.

With the collapse of the mining industry and the decline of ranching as a viable livelihood, the Valley—like its urban counterparts in the Rust Belt and other places decimated by economic change—is a wasteland of outdated significance: rotted tractor trailers sit idly, water tanks overflow with water collected from rain showers, and feed sacks for livestock are filled with bees' nests. Today, the Valley's roads still head toward long-abandoned mining shafts, many of which have been transformed into concealed bases for producing methamphetamine, a drug that has infiltrated the area in epidemic proportions and stands as one of the lone locally produced goods.

But the look of this land—barren, forgotten—is deceptive. Change is afoot. And depending on who you are, how you see the world, and what your place in the world is, that change means different things and offers different constraints and possibilities.

According to the 2008 U.S. Census, Arizona was the fastest-growing state in the country. Like many rural communities in southern Arizona, the Valley is teeming with outside investors who seek to develop its topography and remake its demographics. Many current landowners in the area receive weekly telephone calls with lucrative offers to purchase their typically small parcels of barren land that have no seeming value.

Despite the intractable wildness of the land, despite the fact that there is no trash service, no mass public transportation, and no full-service supermarket, as you spend time in the Valley, you feel it is on the brink of being overtaken and transformed into another of southern Arizona's gated retirement communities, complete with golf courses and strip malls. Residents feel that this change is inevitable, and they dread it. As one put it, expressing a common sentiment, "It's only a matter of time until we lose all this, pretty soon there'll be a fucking Starbucks down here with its grande latte processed bullshit."

He's right. The Valley is becoming home to a growing flock of "snowbirds"—people who live in the northern regions of the United States but who winter for a few months out of the year in the Southwest. Some of the Valley's residents still own mining claims; increasingly, others own condominiums in New York City. The snowbirds elicit distaste or, at best, grudging acceptance from the locals. But a far more complex reaction is reserved for the Valley's primary source of change.

At first glance the Valley appears a place left behind, passed over by the advance of progress, ignored by the state. But the Valley has not entirely been left behind; the global economy has brought it new life. And the boom in new construction is only partly because of the snowbirds' second homes. In the past decade the Valley has undergone a renaissance from an odd source: the border has come to the Valley.

Though utterly distinct from the global cities of New York, London, or Tokyo, the Valley is nevertheless at the heart of the global economy. But instead of basic infrastructure—supermarkets, public transport, Internet cafes—what the forces of globalization have brought to the Valley is the border.

For centuries the border existed as an abstract political and jurisdictional reality, but until the past two decades it had neither a prominent physical presence nor a profound effect on the everyday lives of local residents. The border was not used or enforced; its presence in the community was marginal, and residents didn't need to contend with either walls or border guards. As a longtime Valley resident recalls, "For as far back as I can remember, people from these parts were going back and forth across the border. Hell, wasn't even a border to really cross. You'd walk into Mexico without knowing it."

Ambiguity, however, has given way to rigidity: openness to closure. In the 1990s the United States government initiated an unprecedented campaign to militarize the border. Operation Gatekeeper, which commenced in 1993 in San Diego, California, and Operation Hold the Line, which began the following year in El Paso, Texas, were the two main initiatives of this campaign, the centerpieces of a new federal strategy to deter illegal immigration. Along with building a military infrastructure along the border, these programs dramatically increased the funding and size of the Border Patrol. In the federal budget for 1986, what was then called the Immigration and Naturalization Service (INS) received $474 million, and the Border Patrol $151 million; by 2002 the budgets of these two agencies were $6.2 and $1.6 *billon*, respectively. The number of Border Patrol agents more than doubled during the same time, making the INS the federal agency with the largest number of people authorized to carry guns.[2]

The militarization campaigns did not, however, lower the illicit movement of goods and people across the border—they simply diverted their flow. And they diverted it into Arizona. While the federal initiatives of the 1990s focused on the California and Texas sections of the border, they left untouched the 370 miles of the Arizona border. This included the 260-mile-long Tucson Sector, one of nine segments that the Border Patrol has divided the southern border into, which includes the Valley. It was the Valley specifically, with its unforgiving desert terrain, that came to be the most heavily traveled route. By 2000 the area around the Valley had more illegal immigrants[3] and drugs coming through it than the rest of the border combined.[4] In 2006 the Tucson Sector accounted for 37 percent of all apprehensions along the southern border, by far the largest share of any of the sectors.[5] As a result of illegal immigrants being pushed into the Arizona desert, a journey that is far more treacherous than the routes through urban areas, the number of deaths suffered by people crossing the border has jumped enormously. In 1999, 241 illegal immigrants died attempting to cross the border, whereas in 2005 this figure was 471, half of which occurred in the Tucson Sector.[6]

The Valley itself offers illegal immigrants no jobs, just a route to the promise of one. The Valley is their gateway to the American dream. From here illegal immigrants will make their way to Los Angeles and Chicago, where they will wash dishes and deliver food; or they will go to towns such as Greeley, Colorado, or Southampton, New York, where they will be paid under the table by contractors with high demands for cheap labor. They will go to urban centers with long-established Latino communities and to small communities where Latinos were a tiny minority just ten years ago.[7]

Although they do not settle in the Valley, illegal immigrants leave their mark: discarded backpacks, water bottles, clothing, and, most of all, footprints populate the Valley's desert. As much as any corporate skyscraper, these footprints are the imprints of globalization.

With the steady flow of people and drugs, by the late 1990s the Valley was ripe for a thriving underground economy. Giving rides to illegal immigrants and allowing the use of one's home by "coyotes" as a hideout or as a stash house for drug traffickers became features of the area's new economic order. While deindustrialization and commercial development decimated the Valley's long-standing legal economy, they propped up an illegal one in its place. And although most residents do not take part, some have found the allure of an easy payday alongside the lack of well-paying legal opportunities to make a living irresistible.

As it had done previously in California and Texas, in response to increasing traffic of people and drugs, in 2004 the U.S. government initiated a series of campaigns to militarize Arizona's border. And in the wake of 9/11 these campaigns were framed with a new urgency. The militarization of the border was no longer just about stopping illegal immigrants; it was about stopping terrorists. Indeed, the two were often morphed into one, and the U.S.-Mexico border became ground zero in the fight against terror.[8] With billions of dollars pumping into the Valley under legislation such as the Arizona Border Control Initiative, the Secure Fence Act, and the Secure Border Initiative, a new incarnation of the military-industrial complex has remade the Valley's landscape. Megacontractors like Boeing are on the scene, as well as an Israeli firm named Elbit that is exporting its wall-building expertise, and even the Pinkertons, whose policing of the area harkens back to the days when the conflict was not between Minutemen and Mexicans but between cowboys and Indians.

In the Valley, where even footprints are an acknowledged disturbance, the change has been dramatic. Previously untouched desert has been cut by new roads. Enormous semitrailers filled with giant concrete slabs move in and out of the Valley. The Border Patrol speeds up and down the nameless dirt roads and a set of 98-foot surveillance towers jut out of the ground, their ominous red lights providing the Valley its first-ever semblance of a skyline. New installations support wireless communications in places that still don't have telephone poles. Old cattle guards have been moved to the international border from their arbitrary location at the outskirts of ranches. Once meant to prevent the movement of animals, they now act as barriers to the movement of people. Vietnam era landing strips from nearby air force bases have been reused as material for building a wall along the border; remnants of the war on communism, they are now refashioned for the war on terrorism.

Locals have lots of different sayings about the Valley. Some focus on the area's remote location: "If you've found the Valley," one of them goes, "it means you're lost." Many reflect a dying vision of the area. The Valley is the last of an American mythology, captured in the literature of Cormac McCarthy and the films of Sergio Leone, where the borderlands stand as places with a peculiar combination of freedom and violent lawlessness, a corrective to the excesses of government control and big-city pollution. Importantly, locals see the Valley as one of the last places where one can pursue a life of solitude, and residents take pride in their freedom from the long and, as they say, intrusive arm of the state. As another saying goes: "The Valley is the last place in this country where you can be free."

For locals the border has shattered these visions of the Valley; as the newest saying goes, "We are the largest gated community in America."

In their experience of the transformation taking place, many of the Valley's residents express a narrative of decline. Importantly, the narrative is not just about their community but also about America, as they understand what is happening in terms of an idea of America that they see being tarnished. As residents see it, the Valley's decline represents America's decline—the rise of the border coincides with the fall of America.

On the one hand, locals believe that America is a country with a set of rules and values that support citizens' rights. Locals believe these rights are being abused by the process of building the border in their town—a process that has denied them a say. But it also has to do with their sense of America as place where the government does not intervene in local affairs. One day, during a meeting with local residents, a Border Patrol agent responded to residents' frustrations about being watched by explaining that the situation was a norm across the world: "Have you ever been overseas? There are cameras all over London." The agent suggested that what constituted the new world order was a shared surveillance apparatus. The crowd yelled back, almost unanimously: "We don't live in London—this is the Valley, this is America!" Residents continually draw on such ideas of America as a place of freedom and mobilize it as a way to resist the transformation of their community. "They can't get away with this, this is America! Why are there checkpoints? You don't have checkpoints in America!"

But America is changing. It does have checkpoints. These transformations have made the locals feel like they are losing their place in America. But for another group of people, these transformations have provided an opportunity to reclaim their place in America.

Better known as "Mussels," Stanley[9] has a fragile look. Sixty-eight years old, he is lanky and wears his jeans high up on his waist. The outstretched end of his belt, missing its place on the buckle, flaps around as he walks. Tucked inside his jeans is a t-shirt with a photograph of a fence along the U.S.-Mexico border. The caption reads, "If We Build It They Won't Come." Stanley can still lay claim to a full head of hair. He credits this good fortune, along with his olive-colored skin, to his Italian ancestry.

But while Stanley's hair tells of continued vitality, everything else tells of decline.

Stanley is divorced. He is retired. His daughter is a liberal. And he is no longer in the military; no longer part of the one institution that gave his life order and meaning, that gave him his sense of purpose and self-worth.

When I heard that Stanley went by Mussels, I assumed we weren't talking about the seafood, but a more macho kind of "Muscles." In fact, Stanley got the name from fellow pilots, back when he was in the air force, because he would constantly reminisce about how much he loved to eat mussels and how good they were back in his hometown of New Hampshire.

A former engineer in the air force, Mussels spent his working life as an aeronautics engineer for the government. In his mid-fifties he suffered through a costly divorce that gutted his retirement savings. Alone, lacking financial security, and with a love for nature, Mussels decided to spend his retirement years traveling across the Northeast in an RV. As much as he likes the life, waking up in different national parks, he misses the comforts and stability of a home.

I met Mussels in October 2005 at the Anvil Ranch, located at the northern tip of the Valley. The ranch serves as the campground and operations base for the Arizona chapter of the Minutemen Civil Defense Corps.[10] Mussels and I had each traveled a long way to get to the Anvil Ranch—Mussels from New Hampshire, and myself from New York. But we had come with different purposes. Mussels came to patrol the border with the Minutemen, and I came to write about them.

The Minutemen undertake a wide range of activities, all of which have to do with immigration. They protest legislation, they write letters to elected officials, they go to day-labor sites where illegal immigrants line up to find work and videotape those who hire them. But the most meaningful activity the group does—the one that has garnered them the most attention and that brings Minutemen from middle America to the country's edges—is patrolling the border.

Armed and outfitted with high-tech surveillance equipment, members of the group gather throughout the year along half-mile sections of the nearly 2,000-mile border with Mexico to assist the Border Patrol in the apprehension of illegal immigrants. Although some patrols also take place along the Canadian border, the majority occur along the Mexican border, with patrol operations, or "musters," running in the four border states of Arizona, California, New Mexico, and Texas. The group has roughly twelve thousand card-carrying members, but only about a fourth participate in the patrols. During the monthlong Arizona musters, about two hundred mostly elderly, white, middle-class men, almost all military veterans,[11] move in and out of the Anvil Ranch.

The Minutemen have come to the Valley from across America. Some are from Arizona, but more than half are from states far removed from the territorial edges of America, including Kansas, Indiana, and Oklahoma. But spread around America as they are, the physical landscapes in which they live are quite similar: residential neighborhoods of middle-class suburbia, complete with cul-de-sacs and easy access to the highway. And so too are the social landscapes in which they live: a lost sense of place and purpose. It is to the Valley that these people have come to resist these changes and reclaim their place in America. This book tells their story.

Waiting for José

ANDREA DYLEWSKI

All Quiet on the Southern Front

||||||||||||||||||||||||||||||||||||||||||||||||||||||

"Go ahead," Earl says as he pushes his cell phone into my hand, "just say a couple of words." Compelled by his enthusiasm, I take the phone and say hello to his wife. It's a brief and awkward exchange, as it only could have been; I ask her about the weather in Tennessee and she asks me about the weather in Arizona. "Keep a watch over my Earl," I hear her say as I hand the phone back to her husband.

Unless you have a satellite phone, it's very rare to have reception on the patrol line. Cell phone towers are few and far between in this desolate place. And that's a good thing. That way, even if you forget to turn it off, there's no chance of your phone suddenly ringing and blowing your cover.

But Earl is very pleased when he turns on his phone and finds a signal. He is giddy about being out on patrol with me, an authentic Israeli, and wants to share the experience with his wife. He also wants to check up on her, and have her father, who makes the third of our three-man team, say hello.

Regardless, it's only 6 p.m., there's still light out, and as long as there is light rules are less rigid. The "illegals" don't make their move until nightfall, and the hunt doesn't really begin until then.

Earl is in his mid-forties, younger than most Minutemen. He is a large man, with broad shoulders and pale skin, which by now is badly reddened in the blistering southern Arizona sun. Flakes of dead skin pile up on his nose. Earl was born in Tennessee and has spent the majority of his life there; the main exception was his tour of duty in Iraq during the first Gulf War. Like most of the volunteers, he understands patrolling the border as an extension of his military service; Earl thinks of himself as a soldier in the war on terror. "I can't go and fight in Iraq," he tells me, "but I can come down here and make sure these borders are secure. . . . You better believe those terrorists are trying to come through over here."

Back in Tennessee, Earl is the owner of a gun store. He jokes that one of the perks of his profession is that "no one's ever gonna try to rob you." He is an active member of the Tennessee Minutemen, heading his town's local chapter. Lately he has been trying to recruit new members at gun shows, setting up a Minutemen information booth alongside his store's table. At camp he offers volunteers a discount on their orders, "just for being patriots."

Earlier that morning Earl invited me into his trailer and offered me some eggs, coffee, and a chance to go out on patrol. "Have you ever been out on the line?" he asked. I hadn't, and I was apprehensive about going. He said I had to do it. "That's where all the action is, that's why I drove all the way down here."

Like many Minutemen, Earl feels that America is in a state of crisis. He is nostalgic about the past and has an apocalyptic view of the future. "What's happening is nothing less than invasion," Earl angrily tells me, connecting his sense of America's decline to the presence of Mexicans. "We have already lost California. I walk around parts of Los Angeles and no one speaks English, all the signs are in Spanish. I feel like a complete outsider in my own country."

Earl is not alone. Starting in 2005,[1] hundreds of people, mostly retired, working class, male, and white, have traveled from all over the country to the border between the United States and Mexico. Their goal is deceptively simple: to prevent the collapse of America. Deploying under such titles as Operation Sovereignty and Operation Secure America, they station themselves along particular segments of the border that "line leaders" have designated as high-traffic areas through what they call reconnaissance. Then they sit and walk, and wait, for hours at a time, in order to, as they say, assist the Border Patrol in the apprehension of illegal immigrants. They come to defend their America. Some come with their spouses, others with friends, but mostly they come alone, often driving hundreds of miles instead of flying so that they can bring their guns with them. Their enemy is an elusive and contradictory figure often referred to simply as "José Sanchez"; sometimes he is a drug dealer carrying AK-47s, at other times a rapist incapable of assimilating, and at yet other times a hard worker seeking a better life.

Between 2005 and 2008 I camped out with the Minutemen, patrolled the border with them, attended protests with them, and sat for hours with them debating America's past, present, and future in order to understand how they define and defend America. Who are these people? What are they doing? What is this threat from which they seek to protect their country? And how can understanding them help us understand contemporary America?

I have found that to answer these questions, instead of focusing on the Minutemen's beliefs and attitudes—their ideology in the broad sense—we need to focus on practices. While ideology may have helped bring the Minutemen down to the border, it does not explain what they do when they get there and why they find what they do meaningful. As we'll see in the pages that follow, it is not that ideology does not matter—it certainly does—but by trying to understand the Minutemen through an exclusive focus on their ideology, both scholars and the popular media, as well as many Americans, have misunderstood this movement. By shifting the focus from isolated beliefs to the practice of politics, to what the Minutemen do and not simply what they say, we can acquire a more accurate portrait of who they are and why it is that they patrol the border.

I initially traveled to southern Arizona to conduct interviews with the hope that, face-to-face, the quality of my interviews would be better than if I conducted them over the telephone. Only then, after listening to robotic responses to questions about immigration while seeing a dynamic camp life in the backdrop in which the conversations were not so much about immigration policy as about patrol tactics and military experiences, did I realize that Earl and his compatriots came to the border neither to express nor to formulate an opinion, but rather to participate in a social world. And to understand the Minutemen I had to understand that world. Increasingly I realized that to understand the Minutemen I had to do more than just interview them, I had to patrol with them. As Earl himself put it about the patrols, "That's why I drove all the way down here."

Unlike interviews or survey research, ethnography, based on the researcher's participation in the life of a community, is attuned to the study of practice. In ethnography the emphasis is not only what people say, but what people do. A subtle but important argument is built into the method: to understand a group demands not just an examination of the things its members say—particularly in response to a formal survey—but actually seeing them interact with one another.

To study the Minutemen by focusing only on their beliefs or attitudes, their ideology in the broad sense, would be to reduce them to stereotypes: to conservative, anti-immigrant, antigovernment talking heads. To ultimately understand the Minutemen, we need to place them in their camp and on the patrol line.

On the Line

The stench of a rotting cattle carcass fills the air around our lawn chairs. We're Post 4 on the Alpha line, and there's a large pool of water 50 feet behind us where cattle are congregated. They take turns bowing their heads to drink water and lifting them to look at us.

I'm disturbed by the stench of the carcass. Earl has other concerns: the cattle are making noise. "If they keep going on like that all night I don't know how we're going to be able to hear the illegals if they come by."

Shaking his head at the cows, Earl unclips his phone and calls his wife. He exchanges some courtesies and then tells her about me. "Well, I'm here with Pops and a young man who's originally from Israel." There's a pause and then, "Yeah, Israeli. He's a student writing a report on the Minutemen."

By nightfall the cattle have stopped making noise and so has Earl. Shortly after the sun goes down he gets up. He takes out his thermal scope and surveys the miles of scrub and sand beneath us. Kneeling down, his elbow rested on his knee to give the scope a calibrated balance, he swivels his neck back and forth for panoramic views across the darkened valley.

Earl suggests the two of us take turns with the surveillance. "We can run half-hour shifts." I understand, by this point, that his father-in-law, who is recovering from a stroke, is not going to participate. Earl doesn't seem too pressed to get him in on the action, and the father-in-law

participating?

doesn't seem too pressed to get in on it. Every now and then the father-in-law pokes a stick at the mice running around his lawn chair, and I am reminded that he is with us.

Thermal scopes are tricky. They work by detecting heat, but as Earl cautions me, all objects give off a certain amount of heat, and it's important to be able to distinguish cacti and jack rabbits from Mexicans. He instructs me to survey the landscape, using the scope "to get a good sense of what's there. That way later on you can pick up anything that's different." Directing me to focus on a mesquite tree nearby, he asks me to describe what I see.

I take the scope. It has the look and feel of a small handheld movie camera. I place my hand inside a strap and hold the scope up to my right eye. The world is reduced to a green haze. Nothing makes any sense. I consider how it is possible that this contraption helps one see.

Slowly my vision clears. I begin to see, to make out familiar objects in an unfamiliar way. Things are neither blackened out by the night nor their normal daytime colors. But I can see them. I can see what I should not be able to see.

Earl is pleased with my depiction of "a burning bush, like the one Moses must have seen." He gives a whispered chuckle. "What I want you to get into your head is that it's not moving; if it's an illegal, you're going to see that flash of heat moving."

For the next four hours we take our turns with the thermal scope. When I'm not doing my share I try as best I can to see, through the pitch black, what Earl is doing. He kneels, gets up, walks a few quiet steps, kneels back down, and pans slowly across the Valley below. When it's my turn I try to do the same.

Earl thinks he's spotted someone. It must be close to midnight. Crouched next to his chair, he whispers me over in excitement.

I'm handed the scope by an eager hand and directed to look 150 yards due north. I see nothing. I tell Earl. He takes the scope. He paces around in haste, crouching, looking. His breathing gets heavy. By now it's very cold, and when Earl opens his mouth it releases a cloud of steam.

"There he goes. There he goes. I'm calling it in."

Earl takes hold of the radio strapped to his camouflage jacket and calls the "comms room" back at the camp. "This is Tennessee at Alpha 4." He waits for acknowledgment and then continues in a pant, "I've got one headed due east. About 200 yards due north of our post." Earl turns to me, breathing heavily, "It doesn't feel so cold anymore, huh? That'll get your adrenalin going."

Earl is ecstatic but nervous. What if he has called in a dud? What if he has imagined a Mexican? But even worse: what if his call gets away?

An hour after Earl makes his call we hear the roar of a truck engine approaching. The engine makes a loud, ripping noise. It sounds like a lawnmower that's constantly trying to start up. The truck, a beat up 1970s Chevy, belongs to a man they call "Blowfish." If you saw his face, you'd understand how he got the name.

Blowfish is serving as the line leader. He is the most admired person at the camp. He used to be a Green Beret. They say he was involved in a number of classified special operations in Vietnam. Among these men, he is the stuff of myth. There's an aura about him.

Blowfish parks his truck 50 feet from us. Earl runs over to him. Earl wants to know why the Border Patrol never showed up. Through a rolled-down window Blowfish explains that since there was only "one of them," and since the Border Patrol doesn't have many "assets" in the area, they didn't bother to call it in.

Earl is dejected. Sensing this, Blowfish quickly adds, "But don't worry, you'll get credited with a sighting, we'll put it down."

In the Minutemen camp, recognition by Blowfish means a great deal.

Besides his mythic past, Blowfish does a number of things that give him his aura. Often he'll come to camp displaying a rattlesnake he killed while driving in the desert. Other times he'll make accurate predictions about an upcoming storm (many attribute his prophetic skills to his Cherokee Indian roots). But for the volunteers, what is most impressive about this man is that he doesn't need to use headlights when he drives at night. Blowfish can navigate through the Arizona desert in pitch black.

Part of the role of the line leader is to check up on people during the shift. Unlike other members, who are required to remain stationary, the line leader is allowed to move around. Members on post recognize the importance of this, but they're also upset by it. When the line leaders drive through the Valley, headlights illuminating the dark night, they blow everyone's cover. "I don't get the point," a volunteer tells me. "Here we are, supposed to be all quiet, and they come up with their engines blaring and headlights on. It just doesn't make sense to me."

But Blowfish is different. He understands. He drives with his "Generation-3" night-vision binoculars, holding them up to his eyes with one hand while steering with the other. Aided by the night-vision binoculars and his extensive knowledge of the desert terrain, Blowfish drives in darkness. And the men on the line respect him for that. "He knows this place better than the Border Patrol," Earl tells me later. I wonder if I should ask what difference it makes whether his lights are on or not, considering that noisy engine. But I've started to understand something. We aren't here to catch Mexicans.

Earl and Blowfish exchange a few more words, and as they do the space between them gets filled up by a pocket of steam. They're discussing the Gen-3 binoculars. Earl wants to know how much they cost. They were a bargain, worth around $2,000. Blowfish paid a mere $500. Earl is in disbelief. "Believe me," Blowfish explains, "I almost fell over when I saw the ad in the paper. I called the guy right away. It was some guy who bought them and never used them. He says to me, 'They're still in their original packaging.' I got in my truck and made that forty-minute drive in twenty. I showed up on his doorstep and said, 'Here's $500 cash.'"

Earl takes Blowfish's binoculars and gives the terrain one of his signature panoramic surveys. "That's just amazing," he reports back. "I mean the crispness is amazing. It puts my thermals to shame." The two men exchange a few more words about the binoculars, offering their take on the difference between the Gen-1, Gen-2, and Gen-3 models.

Earl wants to know if he can show me the binoculars. "I've got this young man here with me," he tells Blowfish while pointing. "He's from Israel and I'd like to show these to him if it's all right with you." Even in a whisper, the deference comes across. I make out what I think is a nod and Earl walks the binoculars over to me.

I traveled down to the Valley for the first time in October 2005 and was alternately awed and terrified.

To get to the Valley you drive south on the interstate highway from Tucson for what seems like too long; no matter how many times you make the drive, it always feels like you've gone too far. But the truth is, you haven't gone far enough.

As I made the turn from the interstate into the road that leads into the Valley, I immediately sensed something was different. The gas station at the side of the road was filled with Border Patrol agents; a group of brown people in handcuffs were being lined up in front of a bus; uniformed members of the National Guard were talking on the side of the road; and in front of me was a truck loaded with military equipment. I was entering a war zone.

It's a good thing there's a big Minutemen sign at the entrance to the Anvil Ranch because, apart from mile markers, there is little in the way of signposts. And, even with the Minutemen sign there, you are just as likely to get lost in the vastness of the surrounding landscape and miss the turn onto the ranch.

Coming from New York, I found the vast emptiness of the area surrounding the ranch, its utter disconnect and remoteness, overwhelming. The tents, trailers, canopies, folding tables, chairs, portable toilets, and most of all men in camouflage that made up the Minutemen's camp stuck out in the ranch's otherwise barren landscape, which extended over thousands of acres. It was isolation in its purest form, and this military outpost seemed utterly out of place: an oasis of activity surrounded by miles upon miles of open desert.

Prior to starting my research on the Minutemen, I had been in e-mail communications with Shannon, the organization's media liaison, who had very graciously welcomed me to come to the ranch in southern Arizona where the group had set up its camp and based its border patrol operations.

I met Shannon and was surprised to find that although the name suggested otherwise, Shannon was in fact a male. It was the first a number of surprises.

Shannon handed me a badge that indicated I was a "media person." Thinking there was perhaps a mistake, I reminded him that I was a student and not a member of any media outlet. "But you are here to do interviews and write about us?" he said, framing it less as a question and more as a point of fact. I nodded, and he gestured me to an area where a series of vans were parked, cordoned off from the main center of the camp. It was the parking lot for members of the media, and I had to move my car there. As it turned out there was as many vehicles parked there as there were in what I now identified as the volunteers' parking area. Indeed, there were as many reporters as there were Minutemen.

As I walked around the ranch, I made it barely 50 feet before being approached by a burly volunteer inquiring as to who I was and what I was doing there. I explained, as I had in my communications with Shannon, that I was a student doing research for my PhD degree in sociology. Hoping to parlay the encounter into an interview, I asked him for his "thoughts about illegal immigration." He responded by asking me for my "thoughts about the Minutemen."

hard to maintain

Before I could finish stuttering my way through a full account of how I inhabited the fieldworker's mythic stance of "objectivity," he asked if I had signed in and received a media badge. I took out the badge from my pocket and showed it to him while clarifying, as before, that I was not a journalist but rather a student. As if he hadn't heard me, the volunteer advised me to always wear the media badge: "Otherwise, the way you look, people will think you are with the ACLU, and you'll keep getting harassed just like I harassed you."

I wasn't quite sure what to make of his advice, which appeared to be genuine. We were in the middle of nowhere. Why was he asking about the American Civil Liberties Union? Nevertheless, I hung my badge around my neck and spent the rest of the day trying not to get in anyone's way.

On my second day a female volunteer, who had just finished responding to my query regarding her "thoughts on illegal immigration" by correcting my phrasing ("They are not 'illegal immigrants,' they are illegal aliens—over here we tell it like it is, we aren't afraid to call a spade a spade and an illegal an illegal") told me that I looked like I could be from the ACLU. "You know, being young like you are, and with bushy hair like that," she commented while pointing to my shoulder-length hair, "you look like you could be from the ACLU." Once again, in this empty stretch of desert, the ACLU was invoked. Why, I thought to myself, were people suspicious about whether or not I was a member of the ACLU? Reflecting on the volunteers' comments, I began to take notice of the fact that, at twenty-five, I was by far the youngest person there; most of the Minutemen looked like they could have been my grandparents.

As I walked around, suddenly self-conscious, I was happy to see a group of about ten people who appeared to be my age on the other side of the ranch's fence. They were gathered just beyond the entrance gate. I walked over to them, excited about the prospect of meeting some of the younger members of the Minutemen.

As I approached the group, I noticed that many of them were wearing t-shirts that had the words "Legal Observer / *Observador Legal*" written on them. Having seen some Minutemen wearing hats that said "Undocumented Border Patrol Agent," and having been told that this was meant as an appropriation of "the way liberals call illegals 'undocumented,'" I assumed that these t-shirts followed a similar humor, most likely insinuating that the people wearing them were "observing the law" by monitoring the border for illegal immigrants.

I asked the young people about their shirts and was told that they were all members of the ACLU and were there to monitor the Minutemen's patrol activities, to "make sure that the vigilantes don't kill anyone." A few of them explained they were also members of groups called No More Deaths and Samaritans, which provide "humanitarian assistance to the migrants."

I then understood why the ACLU was so present in the Minutemen's minds and why I did not want to be mistaken for one of them. I decided to cut our conversation short, but it was too late, because from the corner of my eye I could see a group of Minutemen gathering near the ranch entrance, talking to each other while pointing at me.

I attempted to walk back to the camp with a confident attitude, looking directly in the eyes of the Minutemen as I strutted past. I hoped that my fearless demeanor would erase their suspicions. "Hold on there," one of them said with an authoritative anger, "what's your business over here?" With my eyes affixed to the guns holstered to their hips, I shakily explained to the group that I was a student and even made reference to my media badge. A few high-ranking members came over and accused me of being a "spy for the other side." I tried to defend myself. I had no idea when I met the people across from the ranch that they were members of the ACLU. I didn't even know what the ACLU was doing there.

As members of the ACLU gathered within earshot, Chris Simcox, the Minutemen president, pointed in their direction and angrily remarked, "We don't associate with those people. They are racists, they are communists, and they are anti-American." In a panic, I pleaded, "Even if they are, what does that have to do with me?" Without a word in my direction, *multiple attempts

Simcox instructed the other Minutemen to take away my media badge and escort me from the campground. "Get him out of here, he's a mole."

I returned to New York, dejected by my experience. On the advice of my professors, I contacted Shannon once again with the hopes of being able to mend the situation and regain entry. Shannon apologized for what happened and invited me to come back: "MCDC [Minutemen Civil Defense Corps] wants media at our operations. Without media to cover what we do, there is no story on the border."

I quickly returned to southern Arizona, and, along with getting a fresh haircut, I borrowed my father's old army pants from his time in the Israeli military. I had noticed that most of the volunteers were dressed in military fatigues and figured I ought to make some effort to better integrate myself. Apart from these changes to my appearance, I brought a letter from Columbia University's Department of Graduate Student Affairs, which affirmed that I was a PhD student conducting research as part of my degree requirements. The letter, written on official university letterhead and stamped with the official Columbia seal, asked the reader to treat me "with respect" and provide me "access to any archives or research documents." I was ready.

*appearance
*gender

Before reaching the Minutemen camp I passed a small grocery store on the side of the road. As I toured the aisles, the person at the cash register glanced at me suspiciously. When it came time for me to pay, he curtly scanned my items, told me how much I owed, and asked what brought me here. I explained that I was from New York, and that I was on my way to the Minutemen camp. He gave me a quick once-over and then asked, "Are you one of them?" I explained that I was not a Minuteman, but a student.

"Well that's good. For a second there, I thought you might be with them." Before I could decide whether I wanted to ask him for his opinion on the Minutemen, he continued, "You know you just missed them. Yeah, a whole group of them. They were congregating outside the store, having some kind of meeting. I told them to get the hell out of here. I told them I don't condone what you guys are doing. Some of the guys were giving me shit, so I went back in and got my shotgun, and I said, 'Maybe you didn't hear me the first time.'"

Back at the camp, I confidently paraded around in my army pants, my letter strategically placed within easy reach in one of the side pockets.

I was determined to show it to people when they asked me who I was or became suspicious that I was affiliated with the ACLU. I was self-assured when, within my first fifteen minutes back in the camp, a volunteer questioned me about my identity. It was Earl.

I took out my letter and handed it to him while explaining that I was a student. After reviewing the letter, Earl looked at me and said, "Son, the only thing this says to me is that I shouldn't trust you."

Agitated, I demanded to know what he meant. "Well, let's see, New York, Columbia University . . . what this letter certifies is that you are a liberal and that you're probably part of the open borders lobby." Before I could respond, Earl continued, "Anyway, what kind of a name is Harel? I mean that doesn't sound too good either."

I realized that I should start thinking about a different research topic. I explained to Earl, grudgingly, that I was born in Israel and moved to America as a child.

Earl removed his gun from his holster. My heart dropped. Laying the gun across the palm of his hand, he told me he uses a Glock-17, "just like they do in Israel."

I listened warily. He told me his holster was made in Israel. "I figured if it's from Israel you know it's gonna be quality. . . . You know there is no group of people I have more respect for than the Israelis." Incapacitated by this bizarre turn of events, I could only nod when Earl asked me if the pants I was wearing were from the "IDF" (Israeli Defense Forces). He recognized the stitching pattern from those he saw in the military supply catalogues. "Us military people know these things," he proudly noted, "we study these things." Regaining my composure, I explained that the pants belonged to my father. Before I could continue, while pointing to the empty desert that lay ahead of us, Earl announced, "This is our Gaza." I kept silent; it was the start of a beautiful friendship.

Patriotic Racist Vigilante Heroes

Like many Americans, I first heard about the Minutemen while reading the newspaper. It was April 2005 and the Minutemen were in the midst of their first-ever patrol of the U.S.-Mexico border. The media was captivated. So was I.

In the pages of everything from local to international newspapers were photographs of camouflaged men prowling the desert, seemingly a moment away from committing violence. You have probably read these articles and seen these images. The liberal media describes the Minutemen as "sorry-ass gun freaks and sociopaths,"[2] while the conservative media characterizes them as "extraordinary men and women . . . heroes."[3] In some accounts these people are patriots; in others, they are lunatics.

One thing is certain, these men and women, whatever their given labels suggest, have come to play an enormous role in our country's debates about immigration. The problem is that our standard judgments, whether damning them or praising them, sidestep the complex dynamics of who these people are and what they do on the border.

Liberal media accounts suggest that when it comes to immigration, what the Minutemen and their supporters lack is sympathy. If only they understood the plight of the people coming across the border, they would change their minds. But if we are to understand the Minutemen, we need to understand how anger and sympathy can coexist.

Take Robert, a seventy-two-year-old volunteer and former member of the Marine Corps. When I tell Robert that I feel bad for the people coming across the border, his response is surprising to me: "You're wanting to put yourself in the plight of the immigrant that's coming here. And feel their pain. And I can understand that. . . . There have been times in my life when I needed a job. Where I couldn't afford to pay the bills. . . . And I can understand about wanting to make a better life. We are Americans and that's we do. That's what we are raised to do, that is the American dream. Get an education, get a career, get a job. To better ourselves."

Make no mistake: nearly all the Minutemen criticize Mexicans, often speaking of their lack of morals and violent temperaments. On numerous occasions volunteers refer to Mexicans as the "cancer of our society," and almost all insinuate in one way or another that Mexicans are reconquering America; the word "invasion" is used much more than "immigration" to describe what is happening. Indeed, the Minutemen are convinced that they are aiding the war on terror by stopping insurgents, both Hispanic and Arab. But while illegal immigrants and terrorists are often combined into one, and it appears that "José" represented an unambiguous threat, the Minutemen also make important distinctions. "José, the hard worker" is a recognized figure, and he is not their primary target. Indeed, as they often tell me, in no small measure to sway my own sympathies about what they are doing on the border, "You have to remember, it's not just poor José Sanchez looking for a job who is coming across the border, there are also rapists and drug runners." The Minutemen recognize that "poor José Sanchez" is coming across the border, and, as we will see, they contend with this in conflicting ways.

For the Minutemen there is a hierarchy of enemies. And in this hierarchy "coyotes," the paid guides who lead illegal immigrants across the border, are the most vilified. They are the ultimate evil. And it is not simply for the reasons I expected. While I assumed the Minutemen spoke so negatively about coyotes because they are the ones who bring illegal immigrants across the border, the ones who bring over the so-called problem, it is far more complex. The coyotes are vilified in large part because of how they are believed to be treating the illegal immigrants they are in charge of bringing through the desert. That is, the moral indignation regarding the coyote has to do in large part with the way he treats "poor José Sanchez looking for a job." As Robert tells me, "The coyotes are the lowest of the low. Scum. They abandon the people they bring over. They rape the women." In the Minutemen's patrols, to catch a coyote is considered the ultimate goal and brings the greatest sense of accomplishment.

Although they repeatedly speak of "backwards Mexican culture," the Minutemen also speak about the positive cultural values of Mexicans. Just after telling me that he is "afraid of America turning into Mexico" and "angered by the fact that Mexicans don't want to assimilate," a volunteer named John says that "the Mexicans have good cultural values, like family values, that I wish we Americans had."

And much as they talk about Mexicans as terrorists coming to take over America, on multiple occasions the Minutemen speak about how many of the people coming across the border don't actually want to be coming across the border but are being "forced into it by drug lords." And more than anything, most Minutemen also understand the very real, very urgent, and often banal motivations of the people coming across. What we often don't understand, or don't appreciate, is that the Minutemen, too, understand that what motivates José is poverty and inequality, and that, placed in the same difficult position, they might take the same actions. "Heck," Robert tells me, "I might be doing the same thing if I were in his shoes." Far from an obvious problem, immigration is a complex issue to the group's members.

When scholars discuss the men and women who cross the border illegally, they are careful to reflect on the influence of larger social structures. Their depictions of the Minutemen, however, slide all too easily toward distorted stereotypes.

Yes, the Minutemen say that José should be deported. Yes, they say there should be a wall built along the border. Yes, they say that there shouldn't be an option to "press 2 for Spanish." Yes, they say that José has no loyalty to America, that he is violent and dangerous. But they also say that José is a hard worker, trying to "make a better life for his family." They say that he takes away jobs that Americans need, but they also say that he is being abused and exploited by big business. They say that globalization has brought Americans a more comfortable life, but that it has come at a cost: stable jobs, a sense of security, and a sense of responsibility to one another.

Just as the Minutemen are concerned with creating a sharp binary between legal and illegal, so too has public discourse about them focused on a restrictively simple question: are the Minutemen engaging in criminal activity, or are they following the rule of law? Liberal media accounts that damn them make claims about their criminal activity, while conservative media accounts that praise them make claims about the legality of their activity. And from this, one labels them as vigilantes; the other, as patriots.

In the numerous congressional meetings that have taken place over the past decade about the Minutemen, focused on understanding what they are doing and whether they should be supported or stopped, the question has been the same. Consider, for example, a bill proposed in the Arizona legislature that sought to brand Minutemen as domestic terrorists. The Democratic Arizona House member who introduced the bill testified, "These organizations attracted extremists around the country who have a total lack of respect for the law and who believe that a violent response is appropriate to the problems Arizona is facing. The purpose of this legislation is to clarify that in the State of Arizona, the only individuals who have the authority to enforce these types of immigration laws are individuals who are affiliated with and authorized by local and State law enforcement agencies, the U.S. Border Patrol, and the Arizona National Guard."[4]

Legislators who seek to support the group dispute these charges of illegality. In a special hearing convened in the U.S. House of Representatives on the Minutemen, Republicans repeatedly testified that so long as the Minutemen "obey the law" and do not "apprehend anyone," they should be not only supported but praised.[5]

But just as the legal label does not explain who illegal immigrants are, it also does not explain who the Minutemen are. Illegality explains neither José nor Earl, it renders judgment about them; it doesn't tell us who they are, how they act, or why they act the way they do.

The challenge of sociology is to help us move beyond the narrow accounts of the Minutemen, trapped in the twin straitjackets of racism and patriotism. But unfortunately sociologists have thus far not done a very good job. What limited scholarship on the Minutemen currently exists tends to reproduce the simplicity of the media and public accounts.[6]

The challenge the Minutemen pose to sociologists is that they undermine some of the established categories that have been used to define and understand them. Principal among these is the category of the right-wing social movement—defined as a movement organized around an identifiable set of right-wing beliefs.

While movement leaders typically present a united and coherent front, thanks these days in no small part to media liaisons like Shannon, the internal reality is much different. It is not just that rank-and-file members of the Minutemen believe different things, but that for many of them the project of group leaders and their political allies, which focuses on championing a set of policies about immigration and leveraging volunteering on the border into political office, is not necessarily their project. We further the problem when we confuse movement ideology, which is accessed through pamphlets, slogans, and speeches by spokespeople and leaders, with individual beliefs and attitudes. As Robert Stallings argues, such an assumption is a form of ecological fallacy, where "a collective phenomenon (ideology) is used to predict responses (beliefs) of individuals."[7]

Every social movement contains a wide range of participatory roles, and when we speak of participating in movements we need to be cautious not to reduce participation into a single homogenous category. While certain Minutemen, like Chris Simcox and other leaders, focus on giving speeches and articulating a movement ideology, the rank and file participate quite literally on the ground. Patrolling the border is where their work, and its attendant meanings, begin and end. And it is to these rank-and-file members that I believe we must turn to understand this movement.

Many of the sociological efforts that have been made to refine the category of the political Right have attempted to distinguish the Right from the "extreme Right," the "radical Right," the "fundamental Right," and so forth.[8] But such accounts miss the fact that more categories only further the problem of simplification. Instead of accepting and contending with the complexity of political beliefs, the increased partitions deny them, seeking to fend of complexity by purging it. Like the terms "vigilante" or "hero," "right-wing" replaces the complexity of the reality I witnessed with a misleading neatness. It is a neatness that suggests that the Minutemen's beliefs are radically different from the beliefs of those who do not patrol the border; a neatness that suggests the Minutemen's beliefs are coherent. But political ideology—whether right or left—has no coherency, and to search for it is to get the Minutemen fundamentally wrong. To understand these folks ideologically is to understand them poorly.

Instead of denying the lack of a clear border around the ideas that constitute the Minutemen, this complexity should be embraced as an object of study. And when it is, this complexity will reveal something that is unsettling: the Minutemen aren't "right-wing." In conversation the Minutemen talk about immigration in a multiplicity of different ways—ways that alternately channel a variety of ideologies from across America's political spectrum.

The Minutemen, as we have seen, focus on how José is violating American law. But surprisingly, that concept exceeds the boundaries of so-called right-wing politics and includes a number of ideas that overlap with an anti-neoliberal discourse, the kind of discourse around which so many so-called left-wing social movements have mobilized. The Minutemen's discourse of the law and illegality is firmly entrenched in a critique of market logic, where economic profit determines the calculus of human interactions. As with many socially progressive groups that critique the program of neoliberalism, they suggest that the government, by failing to police the border, is selling out to big business and no longer adequately taking care of its citizenry.

The Minutemen tend to vote Republican, but they do so begrudgingly. While they vilified Barack Obama during the 2008 election, they also circulated a petition to get then president George W. Bush impeached. And if there is a politician who is enemy number one, it is Republican Arizona senator John McCain. Quite simply, to the extent that these folks have an ideology, it doesn't fall along party lines; the Minutemen have no place in the system—neither in America's political institutions nor in its social institutions.

If sociologists are going to comprehend how the Minutemen think, we need to recognize how the Minutemen's diagnosis of what is happening to America—the loss of community, the forfeiture of deep relationships to today's temporary economic transactions—is not so different from the diagnoses of Robert Putnam or Richard Sennett, writers celebrated by liberal Democrats.[9] And we need to understand how, even with a diagnosis not so different from that of many of us, the Minutemen's solution is to get a gun and patrol the border.

In Seymour Martin Lipset's classic treatise on politics, members of the right wing are described as "radicals" characterized by the lack of a democratic ethos. They are depicted as "isolated from the activities, controversies, and organizations of democratic society, an isolation which prevents them from securing that sophisticated and complex view of the social structure which makes understandable and necessary the norms of tolerance."[10] But the Minutemen are not Lipset's radicals; they are closer to Robert Putnam's ideal democratic actors.

In *Bowling Alone*, Putnam's diagnosis of America's decline is rooted in the loss of civic engagement and the decline in associational life. What America has lost, Putnam argues, are institutions—ranging from churches to book clubs—in which people can come together and do things as part of a collective, as members of a shared community; what America has lost are Americans who seek out these institutions; what

America has lost is the spirit that is at the heart of our democracy. It is the spirit that Alexis de Tocqueville noticed in the eighteenth century and claimed as the source of America's strength.[11] The Minutemen agree. And the Minutemen have that spirit. What they lack is not a democratic ethos. They are what people like Putnam and de Tocqueville and our whole liberal democratic political tradition want out of citizens: engaged, active, concerned.

Within their narrative of America's decline, it is not just the "illegal" whom the Minutemen criticize, but also the legal American citizen. They criticize not just what is outside America's borders but what is inside. Not just those trying to get in, but those already inside.

The Minutemen say that Americans are not what they used to be. They say that people today are lazy, and this laziness is reflected in terms of their lack of sense of duty and obligation, which for the Minutemen stands as the central aspect of citizenship. Take Frank, an eighty-three-year-old Korean War veteran who was in the Marine Corps for ten years. "Being a citizen" he tells me, "means not accepting things as they are." For him, "Being a citizen does not mean sitting on the sofa with a can of beer and bag of potato chips while watching football—the sad thing is that for many Americans today that is what it has come to mean."

In Frank's account, the government used to be more "responsible": "It wasn't like this. The government was for the people. These days it's all about big business. That's what this whole immigration thing boils down to. Big business. They've got the people up in D.C. in their pockets. You think they're working for me and you? You better wake up and take a better look."

But why is it that when Frank takes a look he does so through a pair of night-vision goggles? How is it that the Minutemen, with a political ethos that shares much with that of the college students who helped elect President Obama in 2008, get to the border? It is much more difficult, but also much more realistic, to start not with a homogeneous set of right-wing beliefs as an explanation for why the Minutemen patrol the border, but rather conflicting and contradictory beliefs, beliefs that, while they include elements of them, are not simply racist and anti-immigrant. There are strong right-wing components to the Minutemen's politics, and there are expressions of xenophobia, but while their actions and politics contain these, they also exceed them. The Minute-men think sociologically and empathically about illegal immigrants, and they simultaneously construct them through distorted stereo-types. Understanding the Minutemen is not, in other words, a matter of choosing one or the other of these beliefs. That is a false choice, one not born out of the reality I witnessed. The question sociologists need to ask is not how it is that these people believe things so different, so alien, but how it is that even though their beliefs resonate with a lib-eral democratic politics, they come to such a different answer about the solution.

Such is the question I will ask again and again. The answer, we will see, cannot be found inside their heads, neither in the form of ideology or a damaged psyche. Nor can the answer rely on the tired accounts of racism. These will only get us so far. They won't get us down to the patrol line, but that is where we need to go.

Practicing Politics

Just what is it that the Minutemen actually *do*?

In large part, my initial hesitations about going on patrol with them were about the prospect of participating—and perhaps, I dared to won-der, assisting—in apprehending people coming across the border. I have carefully trained myself to be a participant observer, but in this instance observation was in fact participation. In that first experience with Earl on the line, however, I discovered something that would guide much of my research: illegal immigrants are very rarely encountered.

Having come down to the border with knowledge of the group solely from media reports, my image was a standard one: citizens with guns, self-made police, arresting and detaining illegal immigrants. The image is mesmerizing—alternately noble or nauseating, depending on your political persuasions, but fascinating regardless. The media has done well to sustain this particular image and manner of understanding this group, focusing its coverage on moments of patrol when the Minute-men encounter illegal immigrants and Border Patrol helicopters swoop down into the desert. Repeatedly, we are told, and shown, that this is where the action is; that from here, we can best glean what this group is about.

The flashes of activity the media and public are so enamored with are, however, misleading if we want to understand what the Minutemen do and what motivates and sustains them. First, such moments are a rarity, occurring perhaps once in every fifty hours of patrol. And, when you do see an illegal immigrant, it usually involves seeing him race past you while you pick up the phone and call the Border Patrol. Quite simply, the Minutemen do not catch illegal immigrants, and their impact on stopping illegal immigration, at least through enforcement, is negligible. Second, our collective focus on such moments obscures the fact that the meaning of the Minutemen emerges elsewhere; it obscures the fact, as this book will show, that the most meaningful aspects of the Minutemen's patrols are not to be found in those rare moments of encounter.

Patrolling the border, I came to understand, is like fishing: the catch is a rare occurrence and a small part of what it's all about. Certainly, when such moments do happen, and they certainly do, they are exhilarating, and the potential that they will happen is crucial. But these adrenaline-pulsing moments are almost beside the point. Instead the Minutemen spend the majority of their time waiting and wandering in the desert, preparing for an encounter that probably will not happen. To understand the Minutemen, we must make sense of why they make a month-long pilgrimage to the border and return, time after time, even when the practical efficacy of such a patrol, as a way to enforce an international boundary, is negligible. This leads to a simple truth: the Minutemen are not on the border to enforce immigration policy.

It is in the process by which the Minutemen undertake their patrols and imbue their experiences with meaning that we can understand the group and what it is that it does. Think back to Blowfish and Earl. Blowfish gets respect from Earl, and it's not because he uses his Gen-3 night-vision binoculars to catch José, it's because he uses them to navigate in the dark, and through that, his status, his skills as a soldier, and his identity as a patriot are validated. And the same goes for Earl: he doesn't catch anyone, but Blowfish recognizes his work.

What men like Earl and Blowfish and Robert and Frank miss, and what the Minutemen camp offers them, is not a place to be a racist—they can do that in many places in America—but a place to undertake a set of practices: practices connected as much to beliefs about immigration as to civic ideals; practices that allow them to reclaim a sense of purpose built into an earlier life of soldiering. What brings them to the border is less a set of beliefs about Mexicans than a sense of nostalgia for days long past when their lives had purpose and meaning and when they felt like they were participating in making this country. This is one of the great ironies of the Minutemen: they come to the border and sit for hours looking through a pair of binoculars, while the underpinning motivation for this is a feeling that in today's America they have been rendered observers, not participants. As Robert explains, "I'm too old to go to Iraq. Maybe that's a personal reason of why I love being a Minuteman, protecting the U.S. here at home. It's my small part. . . . As veterans, we know that serving our nation does not stop when we take off our uniforms for the last time. . . . I resolve to remain a Patriot." But these men have taken off their uniforms; they are no longer soldiers. And in the outside world they are reminded of this every day. What the Minutemen camp offers them is a chance to put those uniforms back on.

The camp is not about expressing attitudes or formulating beliefs; it is about creating worlds. Beliefs and attitudes matter, and they are mobilized, not as ends in themselves, but to constitute a social world. When we look into this world, we will understand that what the Minutemen are searching for in the desert is not, ultimately, an illegal immigrant but a lost feeling of respect and self-worth. Reclaiming those lost feelings is inextricably linked to reclaiming a lost life, and a sense of meaning through the practice of soldiering.

We will see that the Minutemen's ultimate project is not in support of a government policy but is a project of the self—a project whose politics cannot be understood by simply documenting a set of beliefs about immigration or figuring out voting patterns, but rather by understanding how people seek to live their lives in ways that are meaningful to them.

In this sense, to go back to Putnam, it is not just that Americans are looking for civic associations. They are looking for particular types of civic associations, and part of what we need to consider is the way these associations are organized: not the beliefs or interests they are organized around, but the practices. America is composed of civic associations, but they are not all the same, and what the Minutemen are looking for is a civic association of a particular kind, organized around masculinity and militarism, where their ideas, not about Mexicans but about themselves, make sense.

While ideology is not a good guide for understanding the Minutemen, other things can help. One of them is biography. Recall who the Minutemen are: they are mostly old, working-class, white men who used to be in the military. In their patrols they are reclaiming a lost masculinity, reliving the camaraderie and bravado from their service in the military. What the Minutemen camp offers these volunteers is the chance to partake in a specific type of activity that is meaningful to them, an activity organized as a military endeavor, taking place in a predominantly male space, where they can be the type of men they want to be, the type of men they have been trained to be. From such practices they gain something important. Here is Robert talking about being a line leader, the person in charge of a specific patrol shift: "When I'm line leader I'm not really focused on catching anyone. I've got to make sure the thing runs smoothly, and that means concentrating on the volunteers on the line. . . . It's kind of like you're in charge and when its done with and it was a good shift, and everyone gets back safe, you feel good about yourself, and you feel like you've earned the confidence of the people on the line." Robert doesn't catch any Mexicans, but he gets to have a sense of self-respect and worth. In their camp the Minutemen can enact a solution to their grievances; neither the grievances nor the solution, however, are organized around an ideology but rather around a way of living. And making sense of this way of living lies at the heart of understanding them.

Earl, Robert, Frank, and Mussels came to the Valley answering a call to arms. It was a call that President George W. Bush made on October 29, 2001, just after the terrorist attacks of September 11. "Every American," Bush declared in a nationally televised address, "is a soldier, and every citizen is in this fight."[12] It was a call that Chris Simcox echoed a year later, on October 24, 2002. "Enough is Enough!" Simcox wrote in the pages of a small-town newspaper he had recently purchased in Tombstone, Arizona. "Turn off the T.V. and join together to protect your country in a time of war."[13] Simcox was starting a group called the Tombstone Militia, and he was looking for soldiers.

Simcox began his pronouncement with an epigram from Thomas Paine: "Those who expect to reap the blessings of freedom, must, like men, undergo the fatigue of supporting it." The theme of men suffering for the sake of freedom was a recurring one in the mobilization effort, an effort that framed patrolling the U.S.-Mexico border as a rekindling of an American tradition in which everyday citizens take up arms to defend liberty. Eventually adopting the symbolic name Minutemen, Simcox's militia enrolled some of the most revered symbols and ideas of American patriotism in their cause, seeking to establish a link between what they were doing on the border and what soldiers in the Revolutionary War had done centuries ago. Simcox sought to define the group's form of soldiering, like that of the Minutemen of the past, as one that takes place outside the formal arena of the military, connected to defending the nation, not a particular state policy: the Minuteman is a soldier of the nation, not of the state; his regiment is a militia mandated by the people, not a platoon sanctioned by the government.

Framed in the post-9/11 discourse of America being under attack from terrorists, a discourse the state had itself promoted to further militarize the border, the mobilization effort was filled with indictments of the government for failing to protect America by failing to "secure the border."[14] Simcox turned the state's own language against it. "The bottom line," he wrote, is that "The government is not doing their job to protect our borders. I call on American citizens to do the job for them. . . . It is time we the citizens band together to show our inept Homeland Security Department a thing or two about how to protect National security and the sovereignty of our Democratic Republic." Patrolling the border was a right granted to all citizens, Simcox argued, and was about taking the initiative to do what the state had failed to do. "It is time to help out our constitution by acting on the liberties and powers it gives us, the citizens, to come to the aid of our republic in times of duress."

While the Minutemen used the rhetoric of the nation, they were actually embarking on an intensely personal project. For the Minutemen September 11 was a moment of reflection. Reflection not simply about America and where it was heading, but about themselves, and where they were heading. In coming down to the southern Arizona desert and establishing their camp, as we'll see, the Minutemen were not simply responding to the orders of George W. Bush, not simply defending a government policy. What the militarization of the border and September 11 gave Minutemen was a chance—a chance to mobilize and be the soldiers they used to be, to be men they wanted to be. And while they often cast themselves through the language of nativism, as the embodiment of the real American, the truth is that they are outsiders in contemporary America; social misfits seeking a place to belong. What the war on terror opened up was not just a discursive space, but also a physical space, a militarized space that these former soldiers mobilized around. The Valley gave these men a place to renew their sense of purpose and meaning; it gave these veterans a chance to extend their tour of duty.

ANDREA DYLEWSKI

CHAPTER 1

American Dreams

IIIIIIIIIIIIIIIIIIIIIIIIIIIIII

Ask a Minuteman to tell you about his life, and he will tell you about how America used to be a better place.

Ask Wade, a self-described "loner" and avid outdoorsman, to tell you about the trips he made during his childhood to the Rocky Mountains of his native Colorado and he will tell you, "Over the years it's all changed. It used to be untouched. Back then nature was really nature. Cleanest air you could imagine. Now it's overrun with people and trash. . . . Used to be you could just camp out anywhere. It was all free, open. Now it's all become private, pay campgrounds. . . . Of course back then you also didn't have to be afraid of just pitching a tent out in the open. It's really sad to see what's happened to our country over time, but I want to save whatever good bit of it is left for future generations."

Wade wears a leather cowboy hat, which he incessantly cleans, and is something of a philosopher, quoting Tocqueville and Twain with unpretentious ease. He makes statements like "Law is not the same as justice" and "Generalizations are correct but not true."

Wade is a man of routine. Each morning he makes himself a breakfast consisting of beans and eggs on a portable burner in front of his tent. Before eating he bows his head while seated over a tiny, makeshift table, says a silent prayer, and crosses himself. After eating, he carefully rolls himself twenty impeccable cigarettes for the day. More religious than most others at the camp, on Sundays he goes to the nearby shooting range to take a proper shower and have a proper shave, and then he makes a one-hour drive to the nearest church.

For Wade, a narrative of the self does not exist without a narrative of the nation, and the telling of one involves the telling of the other. Both are filled with nostalgia, telling of change and decline, recalling memories of a better past and a foreboding future.

There are many themes in these stories. The ruin of nature is one. In his laments about the Rocky Mountains the ruin comes through pollution, in the form of not just trash and smog but also people. And it's not illegal immigrants he is talking about, but people in a very general sense. And then there is privatization and the transformation of what he says was once free public space into "pay campgrounds." And finally, there is the account of increased crime and the fear for personal safety.

As he continues to tell me about those Rocky Mountains, Wade longingly recalls the time when he and his dad, having spent a day hiking, took to collecting some fallen branches and building themselves a lean-to for shelter. "Of course, these days, the folks at the Sierra Club," he angrily says, invoking America's oldest and most influential environmental group, "would be at your throat if you did that, coming after you with their lawyers."

But ruined nature is only one small part of the story. Wade also talks of ruined cities. He describes urban streetscapes littered with "signs in Spanish," shopping malls with stores selling people "nothing that makes their life better," and too many highways with too many cars.

For Wade the ruin is everywhere, and so too are the enemies. Illegal immigrants are a central enemy, and Wade talks often about how "Mexicans don't assimilate" and compares "today's immigrants" with those from previous generations, claiming that "immigrants were better in the past." "Back then you had Czechs, Poles, Italians," he tells me. "Sure they moved into their own neighborhoods, but they moved to America, to the new country, they understood they were going somewhere new and were going to change their way of life, they wanted to belong to it, they maintained their heritage, and they wanted to become American. Today's immigrants don't want to become American."

But at the same time that he condemns them, Wade tells me that "The Mexicans are hard workers. I'll give them that. They work more than their fair share. And it's not easy trades. Hard work. They bust their butts for their money. Wish more of our young people these days had that kind of work ethic."

Indeed, the Minutemen often understand Mexicans as being exemplars of a work ethic that the new generation of Americans doesn't have. It upsets Wade greatly when he hears that "young people are unemployed and they complain about how there are no good jobs out there. That's not it; every job is a good job. Every job puts food on the table, doesn't matter if you're mopping floors. It's not that there are no good jobs out there, they just think they are too good for the jobs."

Far from criticizing Mexicans, when it comes to his sense of the economy, Wade criticizes Americans. Wade says that welfare is "good and important," that "it's important to help the poor." But simultaneously he points to Lyndon B. Johnson's presidency in the 1960s, and specifically to the set of legislation known as the Great Society, which included programs to support low-income families, as a terrible moment in America's history. "The Great Society was all a bunch of b.s. The way the welfare system there was set up was that it basically said to people, 'you don't need to work, go have a baby and we will support you.' . . . It's like that old thing about giving a man a fish and he won't be hungry that day versus teaching a man to fish and he won't ever go hungry again."

Mexicans, then, are just one part of the story, a story that includes "youth without 'values,'" a story in which Wade is just as just as likely to indict "big business" and the "government" as he is any particular ethnic group—a story in which he criticizes Americans for having lost their sense of responsibility and duty.

Old as he is, Wade still makes continuous reference to his father a source of guidance. "Back in the fifties my father was part of something called the CDC, that's Civilian Defense Corps, and when he was off duty he would go and watch over a power plant. It wasn't about money, it was about a sense of duty, and he taught me that at a young age." It is this feeling of selfless duty that Wade believes is lacking in today's America. "People are ignorant. They are ignorant about the world, about their own country. And when that happens that's it, it's over. And it burns me up. I have no respect for people like that. I mean how do you let the government go about doing as it pleases and just sit back and watch as your own country falls apart."

And curiously, in this lack of civic engagement, Wade sees a similarity between America and Mexico, and it's something he would want to help change there as well. Wade claims that just as things used to be better in America, they used to be better in Mexico, and that "the Mexican people are being sold out by their president." "I would give every Mexican that gets caught a gun before we deport them," Wade tells me, "and I'd say, 'Here you go, and now go and start a revolution!'" Just as he speaks about America having civic traditions, so too does he speak about Mexican civic traditions. "It is better to die on your feet than to live on your knees," Wade tells me. "You know who said that? It was Zapata, leader of the Mexican Revolution. And that's what they need down there. People like Zapata, like Pancho Villa. But they don't have them anymore."

In his account of the decline of civic values, Wade also points to changes in the education system, "In the 1950s and 1960s when I went to school they had what's called citizenship class. It was a class where you learned about American history, about how to be a good citizen, about ideas like duty and honor. But we don't have that anymore."

Wade also talks about the decline of "family values," and about husbands who cheat on their wives and wives who don't take care of their children. "When I was growing up," he says to me, "the wife had an important role. Being a homemaker is an important thing which should be respected. People today think being a homemaker is a bad thing and if a woman is doing that it's bad."

To understand Wade's narrative of America's decline, you need to understand that his criticisms do not express support for this or that political party. Though he has, throughout his life, tended to vote for Republicans, Wade has done so as a "lesser of two evils" and for reasons that do not clearly fit the partitioned ideological geography of blue and red states. "I voted for Carter in the late seventies," he recalls. "I thought he was humble. He was a farmer." These days he talks about a hatred for George W. Bush. "That man needs to be impeached . . . he's a traitor if ever there was one." The last "good president this country had," he tells me, "was elected in 1817. That was James Monroe, the last President who was a Founding Father." Indeed, in Wade's narrative of America's decline, fellow Americans are as much at fault as José Sanchez, and the government as often the target of his frustrations. "They've forgotten that we are the ones in charge, and that they are meant to serve us, not the other way around." Wade has spent the majority of his life serving America.

The Men They Once Were

As Wade puts it, "I've been a soldier since the day I was born." Seventy-one years old, he was born at Elgin Air Force Base in Florida, where his father was a sergeant in the United States Air Force and served as a bombardier during World War II. "Growing up, my backyard was basically an airfield. Every morning I'd wake up to the sound of fighter jets taking off. I remember my dad leaving the house in his uniform, and just thinking he was the greatest person doing the greatest thing. And I knew I wanted to be like that when I grew up. I wanted to be like him, and like all the other soldiers I was surrounded by."

This is not the first time Wade has been to Arizona. No more than a month after graduating from high school, he was in basic training at the Yuma military base in southwestern Arizona. "It was the normal course to take," he tells me. "My father was in the military, his father was in the military, and I knew I wanted to follow in their footsteps."

Reflecting on his experience in the military, Wade tells me it gave him "everything." "Friendship, dedication, a sense of duty . . . it let me travel the world, have experiences by the age of twenty-five that no one else can claim to have. It gave me a sense of brotherhood, a sense of commitment, dedication, and honor."

Qualifying his comments, as he usually does, by saying, "It's just my personal opinion," Wade tells me that one of the worst things that ever happened in America was the end of the draft. Wade believes that the draft is a key aspect of creating unity—"creating unity from difference," as he calls it: "You get thrown into a room with a bunch of strangers, you get your head shaved, you get a uniform, you are with people from different economic standings, different regions of the country, and you are forced to connect with each other, forced to engage in dialogue, to talk with each other."

Like the other volunteers, Wade's experience of the rest of the world came during his years as a soldier, traveling from military base to military base. For an extended period during the early 1970s he was stationed in Germany, and while moving his arms mechanically from side to side, Wade mentions how everyone believes that the Germans are like robots. He had that preconception when he went there. "The reality is," he informs me, "they are big party people, they love to have fun. We would sit in coffee shops, bars, drinking schnapps, lemon vodka, people come up to you, talk with you, dance, sing, and you talk politics. Just like us right now, you talk politics. It's not 'oh he went with her, and she did this to him' and so on. You have meaningful conversations. You talk about real life. That is what is missing in this country, that is what we have lost. People today drive in their cars, work in their cubicles, get on their computers, and never interact with one another."

Wade was in military service for nearly thirty years. After leaving the military, he worked as a driver for a company specializing in the transport of munitions for the Department of Defense. He often talks with great enthusiasm about his days driving highly combustible materials with great care along treacherous roads. And although he was a mere driver, he speaks about the different kinds of explosives he transported with the knowledge of a chemist. But things have changed.

America has changed. And Wade's family has changed. The military lineage has been broken, and it has been broken on Wade's watch. "Most of the men in my family have served our nation in uniform, the ones I respect the most anyhow." Wade adds this last qualification with a sense of remorse. I ask him about the members of his family that didn't serve and am surprised to hear that it's his own son. "He's a pothead," he tells me, his demeanor expressing a strained relationship. "He doesn't have a job, he doesn't do anything. He lives with his mother, and she doesn't do anything to help him get his life together. I tried to convince him to join the military. But he said it's not for him. . . . I know some of his friends have joined the military, and I tip my hat to them."

As I think about whether I want to dig deeper into what is clearly a touchy subject, Wade continues, connecting his own son's actions to a larger contempt he has for contemporary American youth. "What I don't get is why it is that today we don't see very many youth joining the military in a time of war. In World War II, citizens ran to the recruiting stations to join. Why is it different today?"

If he could, Wade would go to a recruiting station. But like other Minutemen, they won't take him; he's too old. And this is what the Minutemen camp provides for him; this is why it holds such an important place in his life. "That's a big part of why I like coming down here. I get to protect this country, I get to continue to serve my country."

For Wade, being a Minuteman is about reclaiming a part of his life that is extremely meaningful to him, but which he can no longer be a part of. It is about being engaged in practices that give him a sense of meaning and self-worth, grounded in the idea of being able to "protect this country." Wade is looking for a way that he can continue to be our protector and, through that, reclaim the identity that he has lost.

Wade recently underwent triple bypass surgery, "I had to be in a small room for nine weeks, and I tell you something, you should never be stuck inside four walls for so much time." During his stay in the hospital, he constantly longed for the outdoors. "I made a promise to myself that once I got out I would be sure to enjoy the freedom of the outdoors." Reflecting on his participation with the Minutemen, he tells me, "In part, that's why I was so eager to come down to Arizona. I had to miss the first week of the patrol because of a doctor's appointment, but I'll be staying on the whole month."

When Wade interprets his time at the hospital, he does so not simply from the vantage point of a sick old man, but as a veteran, where the quality of care he received becomes a gauge for measuring the extent to which he, and what he believes he represents as a veteran, are valued in this country. Immigration policies, tax policies, and economic policies are all part of the way that Wade makes moral judgments about the government, but perhaps more than any of these, his diagnosis of government administration these days is based on his assessment of veterans' hospitals. "Back in 1998 when Clinton was in office I can't begin to tell you how much paperwork I had to fill out. It was a nightmare, and the service was god-awful. But in 2003 there was a big change under Bush. Don't get me wrong, I'm not a big Bush supporter, but I will tell you this, he did a lot for the welfare of us veterans. You know I got a check back dated all the way to 1998?!"

Although he suffered greatly in the hospital, he also experienced his time there as an affirmation of his self-worth and dignity. "I was taken care of by this doctor from Stanford University," Wade tells me with pride, "a real specialist. He was a professor at the university."

There is much that men like Wade miss from their days in the military. Yes, they miss the guns and the excitement. And the Minutemen camp offers the allure of that. But in the narrative of a transition from a life experienced on a military base in Germany to one experienced in a VA hospital in California, one sees that the military meant much more to men like Wade, and it held many qualities beyond those focused on violence. The military was also a place that promoted meaningful conversation and sense of community. The military was a place where Wade experienced a sense of purpose, camaraderie, and, most important, a sense of being a participant in defining and defending America.

To understand what gets Wade to the border, we have to take account of how he talks about immigration, the global economy, and trade policies such as the North American Free Trade Agreement (NAFTA). We also need to take account of the discourse of 9/11 and the war on terror, as well as the militarization of the U.S.-Mexico border. Together these discourses have forged a public narrative that defined the border as America's last bastion of liberty, a bastion that is quickly losing its strength. The Minutemen have latched onto these narratives to establish the border as a privileged space for reclaiming what Wade feels he has lost. But at the same time we need to examine these men's own personal biographies and how they intersect with these larger changes.

Wade's narrative of self and nation, with its nostalgia for the past, is not simply that of an old man. It is of an old man who spent a significant amount of time in the military, and whose understanding of himself and of the world around him is rooted in his experience as a soldier.

A New Home for Old Soldiers

One of Wade's good friends on the border is Charlie. I am sitting with the two of them under a canopy at the camp. There's a TV near to where we are sitting. It's tuned to the military channel, as it most often is. There's a documentary on about the Vietnam War. Usually the men sit in silence, but the TV stimulates a conversation. It's mostly about personal memories of certain battles, or experiences with the various weaponry shown on the screen.

Charlie lives in Nevada, where he retired eight years ago. He's never once been inside a casino, saying, "I worked too god damn hard for my money." He has an intimidating stare and uses it often, looking sharply into your eyes when he speaks to you. The bronze aviator glasses he wears only magnify the effect, and when Charlie speaks there is nothing in the way of the polite courtesy that tends to govern conversation among strangers. If he disagrees with you, he'll let you know.

Apart from the war documentary, my presence and questions stimulate the conversation. Charlie asks me, "Why did you guys give back Gaza? Is it the corrupt government? It's weak, it shows weakness." From his perspective, such an act is so implausible that he can comprehend it only as the working of corruption, but I tell him that was not the case. I tell him that people got tired of dying. And it infuriates him.

"Well of course, I understand that, but you don't become weak! You guys became weak and it's the same thing that happened here. We won World War I, World War II," Charlie continues in anger, "and then people got soft and since then we've been weak, we've become a weak country. And we haven't won a war since." He shouts these last words. Everyone within 100 feet of us turns to look. His words seem to offend the others. They don't like the portrayal Charlie is giving of America. It hurts to hear it. Delbert jumps in. He raises his right arm when he speaks—it's an awkward motion because he can't straighten it; it happened when a shell exploded next to him in Vietnam. "Now hold on there, we didn't lose Vietnam, he objects." Vietnam is a sore subject and a sensitive one at the camp. "We never lost one major battle there—it was a stalemate and we could have won it but we decided to leave."

At stake in Delbert's fear of America's weakness is also a fear of personal weakness, of individual emasculation. Scholars have long noted the connection between nationalism and gender.[1] As Joanne Nagel puts it, "The culture and ideology of hegemonic masculinity goes hand and hand with the culture and ideology of hegemonic nationalism. Masculinity and nationalism articulate well with one another." Moreover, "terms like honor, patriotism, cowardice, bravery and duty, are hard to distinguish as either nationalist or masculinist, since they seem so thoroughly tied to both the nation and manliness."[2]

Following Nagel, it is difficult to distinguish the Minutemen's project on the border as either nationalist or masculinist; the two are intertwined. To the same degree that these men speak of losing their country, they speak of losing their sense of manhood. For men like

Charlie, Delbert, and Wade, personal identity is connected to national identity, and the emasculation of America is experienced as a personal emasculation.

There are themes running through Wade's account of America's decline: pollution, privatization, crime, too much surveillance, too much regulation, all encased in the desire to be left alone. As he put it, "I am a loner." We could consider these as reflecting Wade's right-wing ideology; there is certainly truth to this. And we may say that this explains why he is on the border. But I have two fears about this: one is that labeling the Minutemen as "right-wing" misses the complexity of their beliefs and the contradictions between them. The enemies are many; the ruin is vast. My second fear is that the "right-wing" label misunderstands what it is that Wade is nostalgic for.

Is America worse today? Is there more crime, more pollution, less family values? Figuring out Wade is not about figuring out if he is right or wrong. To figure him out we need to think about what his life was like in those times of what he calls America's better past. And when we figure that out we will understand that Wade's nostalgia is not simply for cleaner air but for something more meaningful: an experience.

While Wade speaks the language of individualism, while he talks about being a "loner" and about poor people needing to learn how to fend for themselves, consider what it is that he is doing on the border: he is seeking to participate in a world. He does not seek to retreat into isolation but rather moves toward community.

What emerges from these men's biographies is not just a narrative of decline but a particular set of needs and desires, a particular way of responding to the experience of change and alienation—one that is rooted in the practice of soldiering. Their past is central to their present, both in structuring how they feel loss and in structuring how to feel at home again.

By patrolling the border, the Minutemen are attempting to reclaim a different, younger, better version of America and a different, younger, better version of themselves. It is a project to reclaim a lost part of their lives, a project to reclaim their sense of self and belonging in an America that they feel no longer belongs to them. And in that, Wade believes he and José are not so different. "You know, people across that border are probably still sitting around campfires talking about how they lost the war to us." Wade pauses and removes his hat, then cups it with his right hand and places it on his knee, as if he's picturing the soldier across the border. "And it's true," he says, "we took this land by conquest. There was the Louisiana Purchase, but the rest we conquered. They think they are taking back what belongs to them."

ANDREA DYLEWSKI

CHAPTER 2

Camp Vigilance

||||||||||||||||||||||||||

FOR A HAPPY-GO-LUCKY GUY, Floyd is taking this very seriously. His eyes are rolled up to the top of his head as he stares blankly at the ceiling. But it's not that he's nervous; Floyd likes doing this. He just doesn't want to make a mistake.

Tapping his feet, Floyd gives a quick glance at the screen, just to make sure he's got the words right, and then back to the guitar player. At this point Floyd's totally overshadowing him. It was supposed to be a duet. But this is Floyd's show.

The truth is, Floyd doesn't need to look at the screen; he knows this one by heart. It's Hank Williams, his favorite. And it's "Lovesick Blues." He chose it himself. "I hate to think it all o-o-ver." His voice cracks a bit, but he carries on in earnestness, "I've lost my heart it see-ee-eems. I've grown so used to you some-how. Well, I'm nobody's sugar daddy now."

Floyd reaches into his pant pocket. He takes out his harmonica. I was wondering when he would do it. Mussels and I give him a thumbs up. Harmonica in hand, Floyd gestures to the guitar player for permission, gets it, and belts out a few chords. Tapping his harmonica on the palm of his hand, Floyd finishes it off, "And I'm lo-o-onesome. I got the lovesick blu-u-uessss . . ."

Floyd misses the Minutemen camp in New Mexico. That's where he started his "tour of duty" earlier in the month. Like some of the other volunteers, he'll split the month between the different Minutemen camps. He began in New Mexico, now it's Arizona, and later it's off to California for the final week.

Back in New Mexico they had campfires and Floyd would spend hours playing his harmonica while other volunteers would sing and dance. "There was one fellow there, a guy by the name of Hank, and he played the spoons," he giddily retells. "We would do these great duets for everyone." Seventy years old, Floyd lives on seventy acres of lush green forest in northeastern New Hampshire. When he's not talking about immigration, he's talking about his land. The trees, the nearby lake, the hammock where he likes to read while sipping on iced tea. And the acres upon acres of grass that he has to mow. "But I'll tell you one thing," he adds after lobbing another complaint about all the land he has to tend to back home, "I'm never going to let an illegal touch it. I'd rather break my back doing it than hire one of them."

Floyd has pasty white skin and even whiter hair. He has dentures and a hearing aid and is unabashed about either. Sometimes when he gets excited, which he is prone to doing, his dentures pop out. Without even a trace of embarrassment he clutches them in his hand and puts them back in their place. His dealings with his dentures betray his obsession with hygiene; he keeps a comb in his front pocket, and seemingly every time you see him he's either working his ears with cotton swabs or his teeth with a toothbrush.

It's Saturday evening and the nearby Veterans of Foreign Wars (VFW) post, Post 120279, is having its weekly dinner. It's hard to get a home-cooked meal around here, and some of the volunteers go to the VFW on Saturday nights. Floyd and Mussels have been talking about it since yesterday, and they invite me to join them. Dinner starts at 5.30.

VFW Post 120279 is located a mere thirty-minute drive from the Minutemen camp, affectionately known as Camp Vigilance.[1] The single-story wooden shack is easily overlooked, and you're better suited to look out for the propellers of the Cobra helicopter that's parked on the side of the paved lot. They got the helicopter five years ago after members pooled their money together and collectively built a concrete platform on which it could rest. Parked outside at all times, the helicopter is at once a symbol of the American military and the communal spirit of this establishment. But it's also a symbol of the soldiers these men once were but no longer are. It's a symbol of these men's decline—an instrument of war, sitting idly, no longer in use.

Established in 1970, Post 120279 is one of the eighty thousand such posts around the world. The VFW was itself set up in the early twentieth century, an outgrowth of a set of local veterans organizations that date back to the nineteenth century. Dedicated to the concerns of veterans, the VFW operates as a kind of union, advocating on their behalf on issues ranging from medical coverage to job placement. But beyond this, the VFW is meaningful for the community it helps establish among these veterans, providing a space for them to get together to drink some cheap beer and share stories and concerns.

As I park my car outside the VFW, Floyd skips out of the front entrance, swinging through the poorly hinged door that reads "Welcome Home."

"Hey Harel!" he calls as he gives himself an excited knee slap. "Oh boy, it's terrific in there, they've got meatloaf and mashed potatoes and a live band going. Hurry up and get on in there." He gives my shoulders a friendly jostle. "Stanley is in there, we were wondering if you'd be coming. I'll be back in just a sec."

I gather my jacket but do so slowly because I see Floyd opening up the glove compartment of his car. I suspect that he's either taking or putting back a hand gun. Instead, he takes out a tooth brush. I watch him as he gives his dentures a dry scrub.

Expecting excitement and energy, I enter to see a slow-paced group of old men hunched over a set of long wooden tables spooning mashed potatoes into their mouths. It's a dark and smoky scene: lit cigarettes idle in ashtrays next to mugs of beer; flags and medals adorn the walls; and apart from the middle-aged woman who's standing behind the bar, it's all old men. I survey the place and find Mussels waving his hand up in the air. "Over here," he mouths.

As I make my way toward Mussels, I can't help but think of Robert Putnam's laments about the decline of VFWs. In *Bowling Alone*, VFWs provide one of Putnam's central points of reference for the collapse of civic life in America, and the American community more broadly. Focusing on one in suburban Chicago, Putnam documents how the once bustling organization, which served as the hub of communal life, declined in membership to such a degree that it was having trouble staying afloat. Indeed, across America, VFWs have been shutting their doors at an increasing rate. People no longer spend time in such places, and Putnam sees this as a crisis.

For Putnam, the decline of places like VFWs has lead to a decline in what he and other sociologists call "social capital." The term refers to connections and relationships that people have outside of their immediate families, relationships that Putnam argues form the center piece of a healthy community because they serve as a resource base for people, providing them with financial and emotional support. As places like VFWs have declined, Putnam says, our social capital has declined, and so too have our meaningful relationships.

But as a long-bearded man turns to me to ask if I'm a veteran, and I consider the gravy caught up in his beard, I wonder about the extent to which Post 120279 can provide the Minutemen with what they are searching for. As my eyes move from one lonely man to another, sipping beer and taking drags from cigarette after cigarette, I wonder what Putnam saw to appreciate in the VFW and whether people like Floyd and Mussels see it too.

When I begin to answer the bearded man, Floyd comes up from behind. With a hand over my shoulder he tells the man that I'm his guest. "Well, then you better sign him in."

Floyd and I walk back to the entrance where a cheap spiral notebook sits opened up atop an even cheaper wooden desk. Floyd takes hold of a pen that's tied to the notebook by a string. Under the column reading "Guest" he writes my name, under "Sponsor" his own, and finally he adds the date. I now occupy the space below a Matt Murphy. Although a mere line apart, three months separate our visits.

Floyd and I take a place on the wooden bench beside Mussels. To my surprise we are the only Minutemen there. I know of other volunteers who had gone to the VFW, and I was expecting a larger turnout. This is, after all, a space built for them. This is, as the sign on the front door read, their "home."

At the bar I order the three-dollar dinner as well as a two-dollar pitcher of beer, which I carry over to our table with a set of chilled mugs.

Words are not exchanged frequently—not just among the Minutemen, but among the entire group of veterans who are gathered at the VFW. They are all from the Valley, and they all know one another. But there is little in the way of talk. And what talk there is comes less in the form of dialogue and more in the form of witty quips.

The only thing that breaks the silence is the singing coming from the front of the room. It's an unshaven, long-haired man wearing tight jeans, leather boots, and a cowboy hat. An electric guitar is strapped around his shoulder. Next to him is a karaoke machine, complete with an old monitor that provides the lyrics and a set of speakers that provide the background music. Country hits play one after another, and the long-haired man provides accompaniment with his guitar and voice.

The men watch him play. While they appear to enjoy the music, it seems its function is more to break the awkward silence. If it wasn't for this long-haired man, this could easily pass as a funeral. And from the downtrodden looks of the gathered men, it might as well be; this is *their* funeral.

Floyd's enthusiasm is a contrast to the otherwise sedate group of men. He is particularly piqued by the guitar player. Floyd makes his way to him with excitement, only to return dejected. The guitar player turned down his request to play a few songs.

Turning his attention to the bartender, Floyd asks her for a dance. "Maybe later on, darling," she answers back. Determined to get Floyd his chance, in part because I want him to have the pleasure, in part because I want to endear myself to him and help build his trust, I walk up to the guitar player and think up a lie. I tell him that Floyd is a good friend of my father's. I tell him that they served together. I tell him that I came down to Arizona to visit him and that it would make my trip if he could have a go at it. The guitar player gives Floyd a glance and then turns to me. "All right then."

Floyd skips his way back to our table with a wide smile. A man from the other end of our table shouts over his memory of the time he saw Hank Williams perform in concert. The two reminisce about the long gone days when Hank Williams, Carl Perkins, and Johnny Cash occupied the radio waves. "It wasn't this crap that passes for music these days," the man yells down the table. "Well, it's just another part of how this country is going down the toilet," Floyd yells back. The men exchange sighs.

For the next hour we sip our beers. Every now and then I ask the two of them some questions. But for the most part I let what conversation there is run its natural course. When Floyd and Mussels do talk, it's about the camp and the patrols. They talk about their experiences on the line, about the different personalities they've encountered, and about the good and bad things in the organization.

At 7:30 Mussels looks at his watch, reports the time, and tells Floyd that they should get going: "If we're going to go on the morning shift we better rest up." The three of us finish our beers, Floyd gives a cheerful good-bye to the bartender, and we make our way out the front door and head toward Camp Vigilance. And as we drive away from the "welcome home" sign and toward the camp, I realize just what the Minutemen's project is all about: finding a new home for old heroes.

In many ways Post 120279 is similar to the Minutemen's camp—a guarded space set up for veterans. But there is a drastic difference.

I don't doubt that the relationships formed at Post 120279 among the locals offer them a set of resources; that it builds their "social capital," as Putnam would have it. But the Minutemen are not in search of social capital. They want something more. And Post 120279 can't provide them with what they are looking for. For that they need Camp Vigilance.

Putnam's work on the decline in associational life in America follows in the footsteps of Jurgen Habermas's analysis of what he calls the decline of the "public sphere."[2] For Habermas, the eighteenth century saw the rise of public places, the pillar example being the coffeehouse, where private individuals gathered to discuss and debate. This was both an open space and a critical space. In the ideal public sphere, no matter their class standing, the people who gathered there were equals, and through equal exchange they developed a set of ideas that engaged the state in a critical way. For Habermas, engaging in such "communicative action" is the essence of democratic politics, and the conditions of political life can be measured by the conditions of this communication—how open it is, how equal its participants are. Over time, Habermas argues, as mass media grew, this culture of debate, and the stock of critical knowledge that resulted from it, declined, and with it, democracy.

This tradition of analysis has been picked up by people like Nina Eliasoph, who analyzes the interactional dynamics of political talk.[3] In Eliasoph's account, Americans tend to "avoid politics" because it is considered inappropriate. Here politics is understood as particular topics of conversation. When "political" topics come up, Americans make efforts to shift the conversation into less political subjects, and in so doing strategically "produce apathy in everyday life."

What links the work of Habermas, Putnam, and Eliasoph is a focus on politics as conversation. To be political is to inhabit a place, a public sphere, and engage one another in debate. It is a fundamentally discursive understanding of the political and the space in which the political takes place.

Such an understanding misses a crucial dimension of political life, a dimension that the Minutemen camp helps us understand. No matter how much they engage in talk, no matter how political the content of that talk may be, there will still be something missing for the Minutemen; they will not be engaged in the types of practices that would give them the meaning they want and need. It's not that the Minutemen don't engage in conversations about political issues and debate the merits of different ideas and policies. And it's not that they don't value these conversations. But Camp Vigilance allows them a chance to do more—to do something that Habermas's eighteenth-century cafes and Putnam's twentieth-century VFWs do not allow them to do.

What these men seek out in the desert, and what VFW Post 120279 cannot provide for them, is not simply a place to talk, but a place to act. The meaning they are searching for cannot be found inside the VFW. In their camp and on the patrol line, they are struggling to create something that the other men in the VFW do not have, to do something that the other men do not do when they sit, smoking cigarettes and drinking beer, and listen to a bearded man play music.

Certainly Floyd found joy in the chance to play his harmonica and sing some Hank Williams. He found more joy in his experience at the VFW than the gathered locals did. But that joy was not a product of the VFW itself, it was a product of a meaningfulness he brought with him into that space. It was a product of the meaningfulness he had at the camp, which he carried with him when he skipped through those rickety doors.

As 7.30 p.m. approached and Floyd and Mussels became anxious to return to the camp so they could get enough sleep before the next morning's patrol, what became apparent to me was that the present meaning was not to be found within anything happening at the VFW, but back at Camp Vigilance.

VFWs are not just places to drink beer and eat a hot meal, much as those are probably two of their most significant activities. They are also, as Putnam shows, places where members once held wedding banquets, where they organized community meetings, held dances, and played bingo. But these are not the practices the Minutemen are looking for, and this is not the kind of associational space they seek out.

On the one hand, the Minutemen validate Putnam's diagnosis. But they also force us to reconsider it. It's not that civic associations have declined but that particular types of civic associations have declined. What the Minutemen are looking for is not associational life but a particular form of associational life: they are looking for male spaces, spaces where they can carry guns and be soldiers at war, spaces where the way they have learned to be in the world through previous life experiences makes sense. For that they need an associational space where they can realize a way of being in the world that they value and can attain a sense of self-worth. The Minutemen want to have respect and meaning in their lives, no more and no less, and the VFW cannot give it to them. The Minutemen are looking for a place where they can be the men they once were, not a place that reminds them of the men they longer are.

Setting the Stage

"Welcome Minutemen" reads the sign at the gated entrance to the Anvil Ranch. The normally nondescript ranch, whose infrastructure consists of a few underwhelming wooden structures and an array of farming equipment, and whose population is dominated by cattle, not humans, has been transformed today. Today is opening day of Operation Stand Your Ground, the first of the two thirty-day border musters the Minutemen will hold this year. Today, and for the next month, the Anvil Ranch will be transformed into Camp Vigilance.

I am standing next to Susan. She is in charge of registration, and the two of us are waiting to greet volunteers as they enter the ranch. Some volunteers arrived yesterday, but most are coming in today. Others will trickle in throughout the month.

It's eight in the morning and the sun is already beating on us. A number of flags are flapping next to us, the strong desert winds nearly lifting them out of the ground. There is the U.S. flag, but then also various state flags that volunteers have brought with them, representing the places from which they've come: Arizona, California, Oklahoma, Nevada. Then there are flags bearing the insignia of military regiments in which volunteers have served. Finally there is the legendary Gadsden flag, with the famous words "DON'T TREAD ON ME" written below a depiction of a rattlesnake coiled and ready to strike. The flag stands as a prominent symbol of American patriotism, particularly among military men who have strong claims and affinities to it because it is said to have been the first flag American soldiers ever carried into battle. And because of this, when the Gadsden flag begins to fall sideways, Susan quickly asks me to give it a tug into the ground and ensure it's given its proper standing.

"Let's see if this is one of us." Susan and I keep our eyes affixed on Don's truck as it shimmies up the dirt road entrance to the camp, kicking up a cloud of dust.

Don lowers the window of his black sports utility vehicle and a blast of air-conditioning escapes. Susan greets him with a very cheerful hello and asks if he's a Minuteman. Don responds with a "Hi there," and a "Yes ma'am." "Where are you getting from?" Susan asks. "Just a little ways up the road, a place called Utah." The three of us laugh.

Don flashes his Minutemen badge; he's already been registered back home. The badge is a laminated card with a photo of a Minutemen soldier from the Revolutionary War, with uniform, hat, and all, except that instead of a rifle, he's got a pair of binoculars in his hand. On top it reads "Minutemen Civil Defense Corps," and on the bottom it has Don's name and address. Susan tells him what she tells all volunteers: "Well, we're happy to have you."

It's a long drive to the Minutemen campground. It took Don four days. He drove instead of flying so that he could bring his guns with him. Don explains that you can check in your guns when you fly, but since September 11th there are so many regulations that it's too much of a hassle. He points out that they didn't even let Tim, a police officer from upstate New York, or simply "Tim the cop," as he's known around camp, board the plane with his gun. "That's just crazy."

The journey from Utah to Arizona can be done faster than the four days it took Don, but he did some sightseeing on the way. He enjoyed the trip, but it was bittersweet because his wife wasn't with him. They do everything together, especially since their kids, now grown up, have left the house. But Don doesn't think the border is a place for women. "Too dangerous" he tells me, and adds, "anyway, it's not her kind of thing."

Susan instructs Don as to where he can park his car. He's brought a tent to camp out in. He can pick out a spot to his liking—anywhere that hasn't already been taken. Preferably close to the other tents. He should try to stay away from the RVs, since they tend to make a lot of noise with their generators. Susan invites him to grab a hamburger from the barbecue but cautions that he should get settled quickly. The opening ceremony will start in about one hour.

The first day of every patrol muster begins with an opening ceremony. A wooden stage is set up in the middle of the camp, and members of the Minutemen leadership and invited speakers take their turns giving speeches. Among others, today we have Don Goldwater, nephew of former Republican presidential nominee Barry Goldwater, and Michelle, president of a group called Mothers Against Illegal Aliens.

The volunteers gather in front. It's a sea of bearded men with baseball caps sitting on lawn chairs. Most are wearing shirts that indicate their membership in the Minutemen; others, that indicate their views on politics: "I Hate My Government but Love My Country"; "What Part of Illegal Don't You Understand?" Nearly everyone has a gun holstered to his hips. Most are wearing at least one article of military fatigues. But they've been instructed to keep it toned down, especially today. Today is the day this space in the desert is the most public it will ever be: it's the day the public face of the group will be established, and volunteers have been told in communications leading up to the event not to wear things that will give off the wrong impression—the impression that they are racists, that they are vigilantes. In part that means not wearing excessive amounts of camouflage. As Susan explains to me, "The media is looking out for that one photo op of someone dressed in full camo so they can say, 'Told you so.'" The Minutemen are seeking to send out a different set of messages, ones that contend with the understanding of them as racists and instead cast themselves as unbiased, patriotic Americans. And while such a battle over image and meaning will be waged throughout the monthlong border muster, the stakes are highest on opening days.

At the start of the opening ceremony an American flag is raised on a 50-foot pole in the middle of the camp. It will remain there throughout the month. It's a different flag each time. This time it's the flag that belonged to Meghan's grandfather. As it's unfurled, we are told he stormed the beach at Normandy. Meghan is asked to stand up and make herself known, and when she does, the men raising the flag give her a military salute. A military drumbeat starts up and the flag begins its ascent. The volunteers remove their hats in unison. The camp is in utter silence.

With the flag hoisted, Shannon, who is serving as the master of ceremonies, announces the "liberty lantern." A small, oil-filled lantern is lit, raised on a staff, and placed next to the flag. It will remain there, lit, until the muster is over. The lantern, as the audience of volunteers and media are told, is meant to signal the "shining of the light of liberty. To watch over us as we undertake our mission."

Michelle is announced to the stage along with her young sons. She bends down and gives some instructions to her apprehensive kids, and the three of them begin to sing Yankee Doodle Dandy. As her sons walk off stage to a round of applause, Michelle's demeanor quickly changes. "I started Mothers Against Illegal Aliens because I am a mother who is dedicated to her kids and tired of seeing what's happening to our country." "They are not mothers," she yells, "they are criminals. . . . They have babies in America and use those kids as ransom for citizenship. I ask you, 'Is that what a mother is supposed to do?'"

As she criticizes the "Mexican mothers," Michelle reads out loud sections of the Fourteenth Amendment of the U.S. Constitution and instructs everyone that, "As the amendment declares, this Mexican woman is under the jurisdiction of Mexico, and not America, when she has that baby here. She has no claim to American citizenship." She continues to make references not just to the Constitution but also the founding fathers as she makes her claims against the "Mexican mothers," arguing that the Constitution has an authentic meaning, which has been purposefully misinterpreted by a liberal Congress in order to provide citizenship to the Mexican mother.

Following Michelle is Don Goldwater. Like the other speakers, his attire is different from that of the volunteers gathered in front: a button-down shirt tucked inside a pair of khakis. "Just like the Minute-men of yesterday, who answered the call of duty, who took it upon themselves to protect the country from invasion," Goldwater says, "we are doing the same here today on the border." He finishes by invoking the Revolutionary War call of "One if by land, two if by sea!" And amidst the applause a Minutemen from the audience quips, "*And three if by Mexico!*"

Chris Simcox is the final speaker. He begins by asking for a show of hands from the volunteers to document the various states from which they have come. "What a great cross-section of America," Chris comments, "banding together in pursuit of a common cause."

As Chris continues to speak and talks about immigration policy and NAFTA, what strikes me most, what I never noticed before, and what hits me hard, is a sense of indifference in the volunteers. As Chris talks about terrorists and drug runners and robotically goes through the reasons we need to protect the border, the volunteers appear apathetic. And as Chris's speech begins to sound more and more like a politician making a campaign pitch, I start to see him in a new light—not as a militia member but as a organizational strategist; not as a racist but as a fraud. And as Simcox talks about politics and policies, men like Don bide their time.

On opening days the Minutemen camp looks very different from how it does on other days. It's the day with the most activity. There are activities that don't happen on any other days. Not just the opening ceremony, but also things like the barbecue, things like giving interviews to the media. Opening days are the days with the most people. But many are not Minutemen. They are members of the media, journalists who have come down from across the country, and even the world, to write a story about these people. But they will leave at the end of the day. And this way, on opening day, this very remote place in the world takes on a presence that few places can claim, but it is a presence that it will lose as the days go by.

Constructing and controlling this presence is the primary function of opening days. On the one hand, the barbecues and opening ceremonies aim to create a sense of belonging among the volunteers, but more so, they aim to send messages to the larger public. In an important way, opening days are not really for the Minutemen, they are for the public.

And the experienced volunteers know this. As Blowfish, who arrived the day after the opening ceremony, told me after I commented that he missed out on the barbecue, "Those are for the media anyway." From this perspective, the opening day ceremonies should be understood in large part as crafted specifically for the media—existing as what scholars have labeled a "media event," an occurrence explicitly organized to elicit media coverage.[4]

The rank-and-file volunteers understand the importance of engaging with the media, but they also understand that there are those who are more skilled than them at doing so. Whenever they are approached by journalists looking for an interview, they simply direct them to Dale, one of the coordinators of the Arizona state chapter. While watching Dale being interviewed by another group of journalists who had initially approached them, Norm reflects, "Look at him. Damn is he good. He is a smart guy, articulate. Knows how to talk, knows what the right thing to say is." Don continues in agreement, "It's from all those years he worked on Michigan Avenue, he knows exactly what to say and how to say it. It's a good thing we've got him."

It is therefore not just that the opening-day events are not for the consumption of rank-and-file members, it is also that they are not for the rank-and-file members to produce. And while they hold meaning for the leadership, they do not hold as much meaning for the rank and file. The practices one undertakes on opening day, quite simply, are not the practices of soldiering, and those looking to be soldiers have little interest in participating.

But in other ways the practices have importance for men like Norm and Don. Just as the events are about defining the Minutemen to the wider public, they are about defining the Minutemen to themselves. They are about transforming the Anvil Ranch into Camp Vigilance, transforming it into a place where men like Norm and Don can become the soldiers they want to be.

The opening-day ceremony, and the set of practices undertaken on the occasion, from the raising of the flag to the lighting of the liberty lantern to the set of speeches that are given, are ritualistic performances, organized around symbolic acts that give expression to, and help produce, a meaningful context for the practices that will be undertaken throughout the month.

The rituals accomplish a sense of community by producing a sense of a collective "we." When Simcox asks volunteers to raise their hands when he calls out their state, the effect is to promote an idea that there is a "we" known as the "Minutemen." It promotes a sense among these men, who feel that they are alone in the outside world, that there are others like them, that here in the camp they have a community.

But the Minutemen are not just signaling that they are a "we," but that "we, the Minutemen," represent the authentic American community. From the flag to the liberty lantern, they enlist preeminent symbols of America and claim that they are the defenders of the values these represent. Their fight is in part a fight to claim that they represent these symbols, that their project is about the values of America.

Sociologists argue that citizenship can be thought of in a number of different ways. On the one hand, it can be thought of as a formal status, connected to a set of rights codified in law. In such a framework, citizenship is defined as an identity that emerges through recognition by the state and is grounded in the rights that such recognition entails. On the other hand, sociologists also argue that we need to think of citizenship, like identities such as gender or race, as something enacted through practices. That is, instead of thinking of citizenship simply as something one is, they say we need to think of it as something one does.

Such an approach to citizenship is particularly useful in the context of the Minutemen camp, where we can see how the identity of the volunteers, not simply as citizens but as patriots, the highest-status citizens, comes alive through practices. Instead of a relationship between the individual and the state, which is the relationship formal citizenship focuses on, in the Minutemen camp we can see citizenship as an identity situated in a local place (Camp Vigilance), local relations (between the volunteers), and local practices (patrolling the border).

Erving Goffman's dramaturgical approach to social life provides a helpful guide for understanding how such practices help constitute the Minutemen's identities.[5] In Goffman's account, identities, be they gender, class, or race, are not essences that people simply have inside them but something accomplished through a "performance."

Extending Shakespeare's claim that "all the world's a stage," Goffman uses terms such as "actor," "role," "audience," "script," "front-stage," "backstage," "props," "costumes," "cues," and, most important, "performance" as heuristic metaphors for analyzing interaction in everyday life. As Goffman defines it, a performance consists of "all the activity of a given participant on a given occasion which serves to influence in any way any of the other participants."[6] In their performance, individuals have the capacity to control the impressions or external signs they give off and thus influence the perceptions of the audience. Through such impression management, which includes management of gestures and bodily movements as well as clothing, individuals are able to establish and maintain perceptions corresponding to the particular identity they want to establish for themselves. The idea is that the individual, considered as an actor, is able to manipulate the information that he or she communicates in order to render a particular impression to the audience and achieve a particular identity.

While the performance of an identity is connected to things the actors do—how they walk and talk—it is also connected to the "setting," which consists of "the furniture, décor, physical layout, and other background items which supply the scenery and stage props for the spate of human action played out before, within, or upon it."[7] In the performance of identity, the setting or stage is a precondition for the performance; without a stage the actor cannot perform. Moreover, not all stages are the same, and particular stages produce particular identities. They create the conditions, which enable a particular performance to take place, and a specific identity to be accomplished, as Goffman would put it.

By controlling the setting, that is, by managing the stage, actors are able to promote a particular definition of the situation, which refers to the context in which the performance takes place and is framed. This framing is consequential because it renders the performances that take place in that context meaningful; the meaning of the act emerges from the meaning of the context.

For the practices that the Minutemen undertake to be "patriotic," the border—the stage on which they act—must be framed as dangerous and unguarded, and hence, a privileged stage on which one can "accomplish" patriotism.

To a certain extent, the state has already done this. The border has been militarized and defined as dangerous, as ground zero in the war on terror. But while the border has been a militarized zone since the 1990s, is not an empty stage, and contains certain "props," the Minutemen also actively engage in assembling the space, making it a stage on which to be a soldier. This involves conveying impressions of the border as an insecure and vulnerable space that needs defenders because it is not being adequately guarded by the state. In large part this is accomplished by depicting the people coming across the border as dangerous. The following recruitment campaign offers a typical expression of this effort: "It is unjust to leave law-abiding American citizens helpless to defend themselves against well-organized international crime cartels and violent foreign gangs, rapists, murderers and drug dealers who are terrorizing our neighborhoods and exploiting the prosperity and generosity of this great nation."

In this way the opening ceremonies help constitute the border as a stage—a sacred and damaged one—and consequentially frame the practices that take place there as patriotic endeavors, involving notions of danger and sacrifice, where lost masculinity can be reclaimed.

The Home Front and the Battlefront

If you want to see Camp Vigilance come alive, go there around 4 p.m., an hour before the evening shift begins. Susan will have just handed Blowfish the clipboard with the names of the volunteers who have signed up for the evening patrol. Blowfish will spend the next fifteen minutes studying the sheet, circling the names of those volunteers who have requested specific partners, and figuring out how to partner up those who have not made such requests. Normally Blowfish knows everyone, and he tends to choose partners based on his judgments about their skill levels—the aim is always to put an inexperienced person together with at least one experienced person. But personalities are also to be taken into consideration, as Blowfish seeks to put people together who he thinks will get along. If there's a woman signed up by herself, no matter her experience, she will be partnered with an experienced person. Ideally at least one person on each post should be armed.

The decision about partners is one that Blowfish takes seriously, but it is after he makes this decision that the real decision-making begins:

the decisions about which post on the patrol line each partnership will be assigned to, and which partners will receive which equipment. There are enough large powerful flashlights for everyone, but those aren't the most important. Even though, technically, the flashlights will have the greatest practical impact on stopping illegal immigrants, what the volunteers fight over is the military equipment: the night-vision binoculars and thermal scopes.

In the meantime, as Blowfish considers the options, the camp is abuzz with activity. Volunteers are putting on camouflage, some are strapping on bulletproof vests, some put on sunscreen, others camouflage their faces with paint. One by one they zip up their tents and make their way toward Blowfish. By 4:20 everyone is standing at attention. It's time for the prepatrol briefing.

"All right everyone," Blowfish begins, "listen up." He explains which of the four possible patrol lines we will be on, each of which has been assigned a name using the phonetic alphabet. Tonight, it will be the "Bravo" Line. Blowfish tells the volunteers that there have been reports of activity and explains that they are strictly forbidden to "apprehend anyone" but can "only observe and report." Then, with everyone waiting eagerly, he reads out the patrol assignments and hands out the equipment. He gives his order to "attend to formation in five minutes," by which he means that each patrol group should get in their cars and line up at the entrance of the camp in the order of their position on the line. Blowfish gets in his old Chevy and drives to the front of the line to lead the volunteers into battle.

The number of people going on patrol varies greatly, ranging from six to forty. When there are enough volunteers, the Minutemen run three patrol shifts throughout the day: 8 a.m. to 5p.m. (morning shift); 5 p.m. to midnight (swing shift); and midnight to 8 a.m. (graveyard shift). The graveyard shift, with its overnight hours, is thought of as the most difficult. Its physical demands are simple, like the other shifts: Sitting. Waiting. But it raises the challenge of staying awake. And while the graveyard shift has the greatest likelihood of encounters with illegal immigrants, the significant difference between it and the other shifts is not so much in terms of the practical impact they have on stopping illegal immigrants, but rather the symbolic weight they carry in defining oneself as a soldier.

For the most part only men go out on the graveyard shift, and these are often referred to as the most hard core and dedicated of the group. In contrast to the graveyard shift is the morning shift. The likelihood of an encounter with José is smaller, but marginally so. The greater difference is that the daylight makes it less dangerous and, what is more, offers no opportunity to use the thermal scopes or night-vision binoculars. It is during the morning shift that most women participate, as well as most new volunteers. For the ones who want to be considered hard core, there is no reason to go out on a morning shift.

During days when the number of volunteers at camp is low, which often happens in the middle of the month, both the morning shift and the graveyard shift are often canceled. The 5 p.m.–midnight shift is the most popular. Known for its dramatic changes in weather, from hot to cold, from light to darkness, the swing shift is a kind of middle ground between the morning shift and the graveyard shift, both logistically and symbolically.

The Minutemen camp is organized hierarchically, and different volunteers have different status. The different shifts, with their symbolic hierarchies, provide one important way that this hierarchy gets established, allowing volunteers to distinguish themselves from each other. Just as going on the graveyard is admired and confers masculinity, going on the morning shift, unless you were a woman or a man with health problems, is often looked down on and confers femininity. But there are also other ways that status is conferred.

Chad is a middle-aged volunteer from Indiana. Unlike most volunteers, he is not retired. Unlike most volunteers, he is not divorced. Unlike most volunteers, his children are not all grown up. He is an exemplary figure of the volunteer who sacrifices. "I look at someone like Chad," a volunteer tells me, "and I just tip my hat to him. I mean I'm retired, I'm divorced, so coming down here isn't such a big deal, but he's taking time off from work to be doing this, he's leaving a wife and kids back home. You've got other guys like that, people who've used part of their vacation days in order to be here. They're the true patriots." The accolades given to Chad express not only an internal hierarchy, one based on a notion of sacrifice, but an idea that the nation comes before the family—indeed, that the larger family, the national family, comes first. Instead of criticizing people like Chad for leaving their family, among the Minutemen it is considered a selfless act toward the nation. The family is seen as suffering at the expense of Chad's participation, but that suffering elevates Chad's place in the hierarchical order of the Minutemen camp.

But age can work the other way around as well. Consider Marvin, a ninety-three-year-old World War II veteran who has had both his knees surgically replaced. "At his age, to be coming out here like that," I'm told by a volunteer, "that's what I call patriotism." In this context old age and poor physical shape are taken as signs of patriotism, signs of a patriotic ethos where one acts in the face of difficulty. It is not physical strength but physical weakness that marks Marvin as a true patriot, as it signals a commitment to the nation.

This commitment could also be measured by the amount of time people spend at the camp, how often they patrol the border, and how long their tour of duty lasts. The main Minutemen musters are the month-long ones that take place biannually. The norm is that volunteers spend about ten days in such musters, and those who are there for significantly more—or less—than this are accordingly situated in a hierarchy.

The "weekenders," as they are reproachfully called by the other volunteers, consist mostly of volunteers from Arizona who travel to the camp on Friday and leave on Sunday. But the designation references much more than the days they come to patrol. It's a moral judgment.

Most weekenders have work or family obligations to attend to during the week. And while these obligations are not discounted, the other volunteers question the dedication of the weekenders, particularly, the dedication of those who are retired. In the social hierarchy of patriotism, the retired weekenders stand at the bottom.

At the opposite end are the volunteers whose tour of duty lasts the entire month. They are recognized for their "dedication to the cause." The volunteers who stay for such long periods are normally the ones who occupy the highest position in the chain of command.

As we've seen, the camp is a stratified place. Part of this stratification is formalized in the chain of command. Those who "stand post" occupy the lowest rung. They are the rank and file; the rank and file of the rank and file. They do not give orders, they take them.

At the top of the hierarchy is the line leader. All are men, and all have extensive military backgrounds. Within the camp, they have the most authority and also the most responsibility.

As Blowfish explains the line leader's job, "The responsibilities of the line leader are safety of the Minutemen, placing the most experienced Minutemen on the posts with the most expected action, and working with the Border Patrol when visual sightings are reported. Much of our post assignments are subjective, and as association with the various Minutemen increases, we are better able to make effective assignments." Explaining the difference between being on post and being a line leader, Blowfish says that "When standing a post you become focused and anticipatory which is an emotional experience. As line leader you are constantly concerned about the safety of those on the line but you are 'in the loop,' which is also a good feeling."

But Blowfish also explains that being a line leader involves great stress. "I mean you're constantly having to make everyone happy, and you're constantly having to worry of something going wrong or someone doing something that they're not supposed to be doing." I ask for clarification. "The good thing," he says, "is new volunteers are placed with experienced folks so that takes away from the stress. But still you've got people who make too much noise, people who are constantly talking on the radio, so you've got to manage that."

For line leaders, the management of the volunteers means negotiating between being too disciplinary and being too lax. And in this there is a differentiation among the line leaders. Blowfish stands as the exemplary case of a strict line leader, yelling at volunteers if they fail to follow his orders and disciplining them for even slight noise.

By 5 p.m. the camp is a different place. The majority of men have left. Those who remain are mostly women, or men who are waiting to undertake the graveyard shift.

There is an understanding that the work of patrolling, particularly the graveyard shift, is not meant for women. As another volunteer, whose wife often also participates in the patrols, explains to me, "You know a lot of this just isn't cut out for women." The volunteer says that he enjoys having his wife join him on the border, but that when she is there he feels compelled to "do the boring day shifts, because she can't do the night ones and I don't want to leave her alone."

But the reality of patrols is that it involves very little physical work. It isn't difficulty that organizes these different spaces at the camp, but an idea of the past, a memory of life in the military that the partitions in the camp are meant to reproduce. On the front lines in Vietnam there were no women, and to relive that experience it needs to be that way on the patrol line.

What emerges from the hierarchies of the Minutemen camp are the ways in which the roles we occupy as members of a nation are gendered. As Nagel puts it, women are defined as "supporting actors whose roles reflect masculinist notions of femininity and of women's proper place."[8] In the battle for the nation, women have a mostly symbolic role to play—either as caretakers or as representatives of ideas to be defended. The real actors and agents of the nation are the men.

In her work on the relationship between gender and nationalism, Nira Yuval-Davis notes that a significant feature of the gendered division of nationalism is the geographic partitioning of national space, both physical and symbolic space, into the "home front" and the "battlefront."[9] Each space is gendered: the women are relegated to caring for the home front; men, for waging war on the battlefront. The Minutemen reproduce this gendered partitioning of the national space in their camp, where the campground functions as a feminine home front and the patrol line constitutes the masculine battlefront. While the women have no place on the patrol line, they do have a place at the camp—preparing sandwiches for the men to take to the line, making coffee in the morning, keeping the latrines clean, and so forth. Importantly, while many men come to the border by themselves, almost no women come alone; rather, they come with their husbands. But many husbands don't want their wives. This division of the masculine space of the patrol and the feminine space of the camp allows the male volunteers to metonymically situate themselves in the nation. They are the men: brave, potent, protecting their home front.

At the heart of managing camp life is Susan. She lives in a retirement community in suburban Phoenix with her husband, Warren. Susan is in her seventies and looks like a librarian. She has neatly fluffed, short hair that she keeps in good shape by dying it monthly and blow-drying it daily. She wears a white knitted sweater and dark blue jeans. She always has earrings and usually red lipstick. She wears beige, large-framed, plastic glasses that have a metallic chain around their back so they can be hung around her neck. Hers is not really what you would call proper attire for patrolling the border. But Susan never goes out on patrol. She takes care of things at camp. She makes sure that the food area is fully stocked with water, granola bars, and pretzels. In the morning she makes coffee. On opening days she brings food for the barbecue and helps coordinate the new volunteers. If you have a question or complaint about the logistics of camp life, you are to go to speak with Susan, who has a firmly established network of other women whom she calls on for assistance.

Susan and Warren spent the majority of their lives working for the State Department, Warren in military intelligence, and Susan in administration. They have lived all across the world, moving around from consular office to consular office. And in many ways they are reproducing their past lives here at the camp—Susan often works in camp administration, keeping track of members, mailing donation requests, and putting together an online newsletter. Warren loves to play poker, and that's how he got his handle. Like his previous work in intelligence, he runs the communications center at the Minutemen camp, coordinating all communication between the line and the Border Patrol.

Located inside a converted shipping container that sits near one of the ranch houses, set apart from the camping area, the communications center is the most highly guarded space in the camp. The "comms room," as it's always called, is a small space. The converted shipping container in which it's housed is long and narrow, and the comms room occupies just one end of this claustrophobic space. On the other end is the registration and information office. It's also the place where all the various patrol equipment is stored, from the radios to the thermal scopes. Even though there are rarely more than four people in the entire place, they constantly need to swerve and sidestep one another when they move about.

The plot of desert outside this shipping container is the hub of operational activity. There's a large canopy underneath a large folding table with a sign-up sheet for the patrols. Next to it is a large dry-erase board, a military ledger, that lists patrol results—there's one column for "sightings" and another for "apprehensions." This is the area where the troops gather before the patrols and where the briefings are held—one before the patrol shift begins, and one when the troops come back to camp.

Sitting inside the comms room with me are Poker and Terry. The two are as different as night and day. In his mid-sixties, Poker is ten years Terry's junior. But age is the smallest of their differences. Terry is big and has soft features. The skin on his watermelon head droops down, his nose slopes, and his cheeks are puffed out. The sweatpants and sweatshirts he wears make him look like he's always about to go to bed. When he sits, Terry slouches down on his chair. He's rarely the initiator of conversation, and if it wasn't for his physical presence, you'd be hard pressed to know Terry was around.

Short with strong, pointed features, Poker always sits up on his chair; shoulders either squared or aggressively hunched forward, he is always seemingly on the threshold of doing something. Poker wears a t-shirt and jeans. His Minutemen hat, on the side of which the word "Poker" is embroidered, is always on his head. A well-groomed goatee magnifies his jagged face.

Inside the comms room is an office desk with two computers, a set of telephones, and a radio dispatch console. Papers hung by thumb tacks cover the wall behind the desk. One of these has the phone numbers of the leadership listed on it, another the phone numbers of the Border Patrol, and another the GPS coordinates of the patrol locations. Displayed prominently is a sign that reads, in thick black marker, "Note to comms people, when you call BP say: Hi this is X with MCDC, we have a sighting of X people their location is X. Remember to be nice and courteous on the phone!" Another sign reads, "Don't get frustrated with Border Patrol, they are undermanned and underfunded, it is not their fault!"

For the most part, the hours in the comms room, like the ones on the patrol line, tended to pass without incident. Every hour on the hour, Poker informs the volunteers on the line of the time. Aware of the absurdity of it all, Poker asks me if I know the difference between "working in the comms center and working on the line." After a few seconds of silent build up, he responds, "about twenty mosquito bites!"

While Poker busies himself with anticipation of a call from the line, reading over GPS coordinates and surveying various topographical maps of the area, Terry spends his time browsing the Internet. At various moments throughout the night, he turns the computer screen to us and shows us yachts, cars, or electronic gadgets that he has found and remarks about how he would love to own them.

Terry gets up and takes down a sign tacked onto the wall. He hands it to me. I give it a read: "To all people on the line: this is bovine in nature, and not to be confused with Illegal Aliens." Below it is a picture of a cow.

Poker made the sign a few nights ago. He made it because one of the volunteers, "that Hawk bullshit, or whatever he calls himself, well he called in a group of illegals he spotted," Poker says in frustration, "and he had made the mistake a few times in the past of confusing cows for illegals. And he calls in and he says that he sees a group of illegals. And I call it in to Border Patrol, and then the guy radios back and says to me, hold on, 'they look to be bovine in nature.'"

As the Minuteman who has the most contact with the Border Patrol, the person who runs the comms room has the central job of maintaining a good rapport with the Border Patrol. As Poker puts it, that means, "doing a lot of bullshitting with them, you know just chewing the rag." Managing this rapport is both the most fulfilling and most stressful aspect of Poker's job.

Poker has grown frustrated with the mistakes volunteers make. "It makes my job impossible. I'm the one who ends up dealing with it, having to apologize and what not, calling BP back with my tail between my legs." The situation is a difficult one to manage. "On the one hand you need to alert BP as soon as you can to have a better chance of getting the IAs apprehended," he says, using the Border Patrol's bureaucratic term for the illegal immigrant, "but on the other hand you want to make sure not to make a mistake."

Poker's frustrations boiled over the other night with Hawk's mistake. And that's when he decided to get some revenge and do some disciplining. He found a picture of cow, photocopied it, and made the sign that now hangs on the wall. He also hung one outside one of the latrines, "for everyone to see." But it hung there only briefly. "Simcox came to camp, and I figured it was better he didn't see it. You know, I didn't want him to think we were horsing around." And then there was the third copy: "I also put one in a sealed envelope outside of Hawk's tent. I didn't confront him directly," Poker tells me in a self-congratulatory tone, "but I am pretty sure he got the point."

It is important to recognize that Poker's concerns and disciplinary acts are made possible by the wide array of actors and ideas that organize the Minutemen's patrols. It is not José who causes Poker's feelings of frustration and fulfillment, but rather the network of actors, including other Minutemen and, importantly, the Border Patrol. The issue of "mistakes" is consequential only insofar as the Border Patrol represents a critical element in the Minutemen's identity. In the moment of the mistake, what matters is not that José is not captured, but that the relationship with the Border Patrol is strained. And maintaining that relationship is a central element of what gives Poker his sense of accomplishment.

Most nights go by without Poker having to do anything other than make his hourly calls. We sit, often in silence. Terry finds another nice yacht and gives us a look. And sometimes calls come in.

Up to 8:30, the general mood in the comms room is relaxed. When the call comes in, things change.

Poker commands Terry and me to stop our chattering. He needs to hear the radio transmission clearly.

Poker is frustrated. He can't hear what the volunteer on the line is saying. He repeats his request for the volunteer to speak louder. "God damn it," he says with his hand off the transmit button. He turns to Terry and me and curses the people on the line, "You know how many times I have to deal with people who don't talk loud enough, don't know how to use the radios, or don't have proper information about the IAs." There's a few static-filled back-and-forths. Poker is able to get a clear account of exactly which post the volunteers are calling from, and in which direction the "illegals" are headed.

Poker picks up the phone that's hanging on the side wall. Border Patrol is speed dial one. Poker identifies himself and relays the information. He does it calmly. He does it professionally.

The Border Patrol agent asks for GPS coordinates. Terry is directed to hand over a paper on the wall. Poker and the agent have a confused exchange. The agent is someone new; Poker says he's never worked with him before. Poker asks how long the response time will be. There's someone stationed nearby.

Poker hangs up the phone. He repeats that he's never worked with that agent before. He picks up the receiver and calls the volunteers on the line. They're told that contact has been made with the Border Patrol. They're told that there are "assets" in the area.

For the next half hour, Poker listens intently to the communications. He asks members for updates. He asks if they've still got the illegals in their sights, if they've seen which way they've headed. Mostly he's in communication with the line leader.

Restless, Poker keeps telling us that he hopes Border Patrol will "get those bastards." Another five minutes pass. Border Patrol has still not arrived. Poker is agitated, "It would be a shame if they don't get the IAs."

About half an hour after the call was first made, Border Patrol agents arrive on the scene. Over the course of the next hour, intermittent updates are given about Border Patrol's efforts in locating the illegal immigrants. As more time passes, it becomes apparent that the illegal immigrants are not going to be captured. Eventually the Border Patrol leaves the scene. Poker is incensed.

Within five minutes, three Border Patrol trucks pull into the Minutemen campground. Before they enter the comms room, Poker turns to me and asks me to leave. Dejected, I step outside. But I know what they are going to be talking about. It is the tactic of "lighting 'em up." The Border Patrol had recently instructed the Minutemen to stop doing it, and Poker wasn't happy about it.

The primary tactic the Minutemen use to try to stop illegal immigrants is to "light them up." It is a tactic transported to the border from deer hunting and involves volunteers turning on a large, 100 watt flashlight when they encounter illegal immigrants. As Blowfish explained to volunteers at a briefing, "When you hear them come, stay quiet and wait as much as possible, wait for them to be close and then light 'em up, try to get 'em between the eyes if you can. That'll startle them and disorient them and the chances are higher that they will stop. Otherwise, if you just shine the light near them but not directly at 'em they'll just keep on running."

But at certain points, depending on which official was in charge of the Tucson sector, the Border Patrol would instruct the Minutemen to stop using this tactic. Over the course of the days that the Minutemen stopped using the "lighting" tactic, the gap between the number of illegal immigrants "sighted" and the number "apprehended" expanded, at least according to the numbers on the ledger outside the comms room. Normally the sighting-to-apprehension ratio was about 30 percent, and in the days after the change in policy, the ratio was less than 10 percent. Many of the volunteers were upset.

But the truth is, whether they use the light or not, the chance of catching José is very slim. And even among the Minutemen, not everyone is convinced that the lighting tactic has any impact. Alvin, for example, has frustrations, explaining that each time he has used the lights on patrol, "they just kept on running." But Kevin, a proponent of the technique, questions whether this might have been not because of the light but because of poor tactics on Alvin's part: "Well, how are you doing it? Are you getting them when they are close to you? Because that makes a difference." Alvin doesn't like the questioning of his skills and fires back, "Yes, believe me, I know what I'm doing."

In reality, there is no real difference—Kevin and Alvin are just as likely to have José run by them. And the Minutemen know this. Kevin interjects, "Well, shining the light is also a way to harass them a little bit, you know, you see them and want to do something, it pisses you off, so shining the light on them is also a small way to frustrate them, to get some anger out." Alvin, responds, half in jest, "I see you want to start tackling them when you see them, you want to get some of your angst out."

Although couched in a humorous tone, the comment is a criticism, and it is taken as such by Kevin, who tries to save face. "Actually, it wasn't me, it was the guy I was posted with, you know he kept walking around, he was all mad and cursing, and I really had to keep him calm."

I witnessed many such confrontations among Minutemen. And repeatedly I witnessed disagreements. It is important to recognize these when we try to understand who the Minutemen are, what they do, and what it means to belong to the organization.

In the summer of 2008 a volunteer named Gordon came up with a new patrol tactic. Instead of spreading across a single line, patrols would be organized in a horseshoe formation. The logic behind it was, as Gordon explains, "That way you hit them with the lights from different directions and they get all disoriented. You know, that way they don't know which way to go and they'll be more liable to stop running."

It's the day after the first "horseshoe" patrol took place, and Elmer doesn't like it. "I don't want to go to jail, and," he pauses, thinking about whether he should continue to say what he is going to say in front of everyone, "the ACLU might have a valid point on that one. Because if we are shining lights on them, from all around, that could very well constitute intimidation, and they could get us on that one." But Norm likes the new tactic, and he brushes off Elmer's comments with a patronizing, "Well maybe we're all going to jail then." Sensing Elmer's displeasure, Norm adds, in a more conciliatory tone, "look, all we're doing is shining a light on them, it's seriously no big deal." But for Elmer it was a big deal, and it wasn't just because he was afraid of going to jail. "I don't know, you could also piss someone off that way, and I'm worried. If its drug runners and you shine a light on them like that in a circle, they're going to be pissed off. I know I'd be. And I don't want to be in a firefight and have someone get hurt." Elmer's critique expresses a set of ideas and relationships. Through the figure of the "drug runner," there is the sense of fear that undergirds what appears on the surface to be a fearless operation. But more than this, in Elmer's account, commonality is found not with fellow Minutemen, whose tactics he finds problematic, but with the ACLU and, even more, the drug runner. On the one hand, he sees legitimacy in what he imagines as the ACLU's position; on the other hand, he imagines the potential response of the drug runner by considering his own response, noting that he too would be "pissed off" by having light shined at him.

Importantly, for many members, the meaningfulness of the patrols, and the course of action to be taken, has to do not with apprehending José, but with following organization rules. As Phil tells me, "Sometimes when I see one I want to just push him into a cactus or something, you know? But leadership says we can't do that. And basically, I do what the leadership says, they give the orders and I follow them." In Phil's comments, the proper course of action is following orders. These are not the orders of the state but the orders of the organization. And although volunteers express frustrations regarding the "laws" to which the organization's standard operating procedures are tailored, they respect the value of obeying the rules of the organization. In such a way, obedience to the "Law," that is, the law of the state, emerges in large part as a byproduct of obedience to law of the organization.

The concept of "vigilantism," so often used to understand the Minutemen, rests on a reified conception of the state.[10] But to understand the Minutemen and their relationship to the state, the state needs to be conceived in a dynamic way.

The Minutemen distinguish between the government, understood as "the men in suits" or "Washington D.C.," and the Border Patrol agents. For the status the Minutemen seek, it matters much more to the volunteers what the Border Patrol thinks of them than what the men in suits think. The status they seek, the status of patriotism, involves judgment about the practices they undertake, and such a judgment can come from the Border Patrol and not the men in suits.

For the volunteers, the sense that the Border Patrol respects them is critical for their own sense of respect, and even the smallest, most ambiguous gesture that conveys that is magnified. From a simple handshake to engaging in conversation with an agent about the ins and outs of the equipment they are using, the volunteers interpret these as signs that the Border Patrol respects them. Of all the sources of validation for what they are doing, the occasional thumbs-up from a passing Border Patrol agent is unmatched.

When the Border Patrol instructed the Minutemen to stop their tactic of "lighting 'em up," they explained that it was because "it usually causes the IAs to scatter and makes our job more difficult." But that's not the whole story. No, this was about much more than apprehending José.

Official Border Patrol estimates suggest that one out of every four border crossers is apprehended. Unofficially, agents put this number at one of every seven. Moreover, as an agent told me, expressing a common diagnosis, "Basically if they don't make it the first time, they try again.

And if they don't make it the second time they try again. Eventually, they will get across." Regardless of the Minutemen and what they are doing, the Border Patrol is ineffective. And they know this. So their conflict with the Minuteman is not organized around operational effectiveness; rather, it is a conflict over the Border Patrol's own sense of status, a status that the presence of the Minutemen is endangering.

Thomas Gieryn argues that communities differentiate themselves through a process of what he calls "boundary-work."[11] Focusing on scientists, Gieryn shows how the differences between what counts as "science" and "non-science" is rooted in a struggle for authority and status. The distinctions upon which this difference is based are not ready-made, but rather produced through active construction, that is, "boundary-work." The Border Patrol's relationship with the Minutemen expresses this dynamic, where agents construct a set of discursive parameters through which they distinguish themselves from the Minutemen and claim authority.

One of the central boundaries constructed by the Border Patrol focuses on technical skill. T. J. Bonner, president of the national Border Patrol Council, expressed his objection to the Minutemen by drawing distinctions between the "trained" agents and the "untrained" Minutemen. "Border Patrol agents undergo 19 weeks of intensive training. It makes us nervous when citizens are out there armed because things go bump in the night when you are out there. Untrained people might do things that a trained person would not do. The fact that people are out there armed . . . is certainly something that concerns me."[12]

Border Patrol agents—even the ones who showered praises on the Minutemen for what they were doing—would *never* claim that the presence of the Minutemen has any impact on the number of apprehensions. As one agent suggested, "Yeah we appreciate them, but they don't make any real difference."

But while the Border Patrol agents are reluctant to concede that the Minutemen have any impact when it comes to apprehensions, they do say they have other impacts: the Minutemen help Border Patrol get more funding. As an agent put it, "Basically they've really brought attention onto the border and I tell you, a big part of the money we've been getting from D.C. I personally see it is a direct result of that."

To the extent that the Minutemen's patrols of the border provide an arena in which to examine the question of vigilantism, that question needs to be approached not through the imposition of static external categories, but through an examination of how the issue of the law and its breaching emerges through a dynamic process of negotiation; negotiation that the Minutemen engage in with one another as well as with the state. Are the Minutemen vigilantes? Does shining a light constitute the breach of the state's monopoly over violence? It's not clear, but what is clear is that it is a question that the Minutemen themselves ask and whose resolution is always temporary, partial, and filled with conflict.

What is being defended in the camp is therefore not simply a government policy, but a sense of self. This sense of self is connected both to specific professional practices and to social constructions of gender. Trained to be soldiers, the Minutemen have re-created a battlefield on the border. This battlefield is a masculine space; inhabiting it allows the Minutemen to perform and prove their own masculinity. They claim this masculinity both through the supposed physical hardship and danger of the patrols and through the ability to effectually use the weapons of war. For Poker, the frustration of not being able to hear men over the radio's static—his explosive anger that the other men could not use their equipment properly—was bound up in a failure of this masculine performance. And being reprimanded by the Border Patrol, by men with actual jurisdiction and power, was intolerable.

The Minutemen camp is organized as a military outpost, and everything in the camp—meetings that are called "strategy briefings," toilets referred to as "latrines," patrol operations called "musters," the organizational hierarchy known as a "chain of command," names of patrol lines that use military code—reproduces the life of soldiering. On patrols the Minutemen put on camouflage, do "recon work," and call each other by their old "handles" from their days in the military; others work in the "comms room." But this life is not about actually engaging in a battle. It is about being part of a group, having a sense of duty, of rules and responsibilities. Indeed, it is about being a useful person. Though many are now retired, the Minutemen speak of going on patrol through the language of labor. Robert "works" on the "Alpha line," "clocks in at

5 p.m. and clocks out at 12." "The swing shift," he tells me, referring to the 5 p.m.–midnight shift, "that's when I work."

I started this chapter with Robert Putnam, and I want to conclude by returning to him. The story that Putnam tells in *Bowling Alone* is not unlike the story the Minutemen tell about America. Like the Minutemen's story, Putnam's is a nostalgic one, recalling an older and better America in which civic engagement flourished and there was a strong sense of community. The decline in civic engagement represents America's decline.

In response to Putnam's account, a few scholars have taken issue with the accuracy of his data and with the reasons he gives for the decline in civic engagement. But almost no one has questioned his embrace of civic engagement as the foundation for a healthy America.

To his credit, Putnam[13] himself hints that civic engagement can sometimes have problematic outcomes. Distinguishing between social capital that is exclusive versus inclusive, or "bonding" versus "bridging," in his words, Putnam alerts us to the fact that "social capital is often most easily created in opposition to something or someone else" (361). But although he raises these red flags, he leaves them in the background, opting instead for an account of social capital and civic engagement that is decidedly positive. Hence the nostalgia and laments.

Putnam is not alone. Indeed, the reason his book received the deservedly important reaction that it did is that we Americans believe in the virtues of civic engagement, and a story of its decline is a story of our failure. The response has therefore been either to consider whether it is in fact true that civic engagement is in decline or to offer ways to resuscitate it. One response is defensive, the other hopeful. Both, I believe, are shortsighted.

When we champion civic engagement as an almost unconscious reflex, as our politicians and educators do, we need to be careful. The Minutemen are as good an example of civic engagement as we have in contemporary America.

But what kind of civic engagement is this? What kind of social capital is produced? And what kind of community is developed?

Like many Americans, the Minutemen feel alienated and alone, and they come to the border to assuage those feelings. But the Minutemen's politics of community, indeed their enactment of community, motivated by the principles of civic engagement, is rooted in exclusion and the establishment of boundaries. Instead of casting this as a unique community—right-wing, racist, fanatic—understanding it might require understanding the very nature of community as an exclusionary, but also civic, project.

ANDREA DYLEWSKI

CHAPTER 3

Gordon and His Guns

||||||||||||||||||||||||||||||||||||||

WHEN GORDON AND I FIRST MET IN EARLY 2006, he didn't have any guns. In the middle of 2007, we go out together to patrol the U.S.-Mexico border and I learn that he has amassed a cache of weaponry.

Gordon pops the trunk of his car. He calls me over. I help him take out the camouflage netting. We drape it over the roof of the car.

Gordon tells me not to worry. But he cautions me to stay close to him throughout the night. "I will protect you."

But Gordon also wants me to protect him.

"Harel, I know you don't have much training with guns, but it's important you are fully aware of where everything is, because should something happen, just in case, and you need to step in, I need to know that you can do it."

Gordon walks back to the trunk and removes a bucket. He walks the bucket over to our lawn chairs and places it between them. I grab the bag filled with sandwiches, protein bars, and water bottles from the trunk and take it to the bucket. I'm about to put our food inside the bucket. But that's not what it's there for. There's a gigantic .44-magnum revolver inside the bucket, its barrel pointing right at me. The gun is excessively large. It looks like something you would have as part of a cowboy costume.

Gordon drapes a sweatshirt over the bucket. "This gun will always be here between us. If they come and happen to get close to us and surround us, I want you to stay close to the bucket and make sure that they don't go for it. I'm covering it so they don't see it." I nod.

We walk back to the car. Gordon opens the rear passenger side door and rolls down the window, the one facing Mexico. It's the direction José will be coming from. He clears away the camouflage netting that's hanging over the window. There's a blue tarp lying along the back seat. Gordon lifts it—not completely, but just enough for me to have a look at the double-barreled shotgun.

You're not supposed to bring "long arms" on patrol. Chris Simcox says it gives the group a bad image, an image they don't want to project to the public. Gordon knows this and so do I. But he doesn't say anything and I take this as a sign that he wants me to be quiet about it as well. He trusts me. It'll be our little secret. "Now look, I'm rolling down the window so you can crouch down, grab it, and shoot through the window if you need to." Gordon gets down to one knee and directs me with his hand to the view ahead. "This way you have a clear visual." I nod.

I begin to walk back to my lawn chair, dazed by what I have just seen. The revolver struck me as silly. But the shotgun gave me a chill.

Gordon stops me. "There's one more Harel."

He opens up the glove compartment of his car and takes out a small pistol. "I always keep this one in the glove compartment, it won't do so much, it's really for close-range contact, but it's here in case you need it." Gordon examines the gun. He's trying to determine if it's loaded. He fidgets with the weapon. He doesn't really know what he's doing. There's one more bullet in the chamber. He wants to remove it and reload the gun. But he can't figure out how to do it. He's fidgeting with it, cocking it, opening up the chamber, pointing the gun around. I gently step back, hoping he won't notice. I'm scared the gun might go off, but I don't want him to sense my concern. I don't want him to feel embarrassed.

Gordon thinks of himself as a father figure to me, and he's trying to show off his manliness. The other Minutemen don't give him much respect. They make fun of him. And he desperately wants some respect. He wants to belong. He wants to prove that he too is a man. In front of the others the odds are stacked against him; he takes orders from them. But in front of me he can give orders. I seem to be the only one at the camp who's got a lower status than him. In front of me he can show off.

Perturbed and embarrassed, Gordon turns to me, trying to save face, "All right, this one we'll just not use, it will be here as a last resort."

Gordon and I settle into our chairs. The bright sun starts to give way to the stars, and he instructs me that if I want to have a cigarette or go to the bathroom, now is the time to do so, because once it becomes fully dark there is to be no moving about.

Darkness sets in and we sit in silence for an hour.

Before we went out on patrol, Gordon told me that we wouldn't be able to talk that much. He said he was happy to take me out with him but cautioned, "You have to be real quiet on patrol so I don't know how much chance we'll get to talk about your research." Recalling his words, I decide to cautiously slip in a question.

Gordon says that what's happening to America is an "invasion." "*They* are the enemy," he whispers while pointing to the pitch-black desert ahead. He says the word "they" in a defensive way, as if arguing with someone who thinks that *he* is the enemy.

He tells me that people are coming from Mexico in order to take over our country. "You know, they think this is theirs . . . and they don't obey our laws, they don't understand what it means to be American." He pauses. The comments are angry but also almost robotic. It is as if Gordon is pleading a case. But what is the position that he is defending with these accusations? What is the connection between these claims and his presence in the Arizona desert? The answer comes as he starts back up: "But I'm not backing down, I'm not the type of person who backs down and I want you to know that." I nod. And I begin to make sense of the accusations. This isn't about the identity of the Mexicans, but about Gordon's identity. It's not the enemy's identity that is on the line, but the defender's. This is about becoming a defender. Becoming a man. Gordon leans toward me, as if sharing a secret. "Just so you know, if something happens, I am staying and fighting, I am not running."

Gordon straightens back up on his chair. He tells me the person he was on patrol with the other night would have run if something were to happen. "He was this old guy, and he couldn't hear, and he was really fragile. And he was playing with the radio all night, making noises, ruining the whole operation. I grabbed him by the chest and said, 'Look here, you gotta quit this stuff.' That guy," Gordon tells me, "was not a good Minuteman. I hope nothing will happen," he continues in an animated whisper, "that is the best scenario, that's the scenario I want. But to back down is to give them our country. There are Minutemen who would run, but the good ones will stay and fight."

Learning from Gordon

In some ways Gordon is like other Minuteman. Like most Minutemen, he is retired, divorced, white, and working class. He has a feeling that the world around him is changing in such a way that he has lost his place in it. And like most of the other volunteers, Gordon's story of becoming a Minuteman is a story of a quest for a lost sense of self-respect, meaning, and masculinity. But what makes his case compelling is not what makes him similar to the other Minutemen, but what makes him different; not what he has, but what he lacks: military experience. Gordon was never in the military, and in this he is part of a minority among the volunteers.

The majority of Minutemen, having spent time in the military, and beyond this, in law enforcement, activities like hunting, and civic associations like gun clubs, have developed what Pierre Bourdieu calls a "habitus"—a knowledge with which they undertake practices and understand the world.[1] Like all types of habitus, theirs is a particular one; through their previous life experiences, these military men have acquired a military habitus.

This military habitus, as with all forms of habitus, makes sense only in particular contexts. It allows one to navigate not the entire world, but a particular world, a world from which this habitus emerged and for which it has been suited. The challenge for the Minutemen, veterans of wars past, groomed to load guns and wear camouflage, is to find a place where their life experiences can be put to use. For the Minutemen, it is about finding a place in the world where their skills and dispositions can, once again, be rendered meaningful. In the Minutemen camp they have constructed a place where they can be who they are, who they have been trained to be.

But Gordon was never trained for this.

What the Minutemen have done is create a social world in which their military pasts can be extended and resurrected, and, in the case of some like Gordon, invented. For Gordon, acquiring a sense of purpose and meaning means becoming the soldier he never was. For other

Minutemen, it means becoming the soldiers they used to be. Like the others, Gordon is searching for purpose and meaning, but unlike the others, he must work to fit in.

Gordon's status as an outsider trying to get in, precisely because of its contrasts, articulates the norm in a powerful way. Because the process by which he participates with the Minuteman includes episodes of failure, embarrassment, and change, his case offers keen insight into the normative and hegemonic dimensions that organize the Minutemen's identity and camp dynamics. His story of participating in the group offers insights into the structure of the organization and the identity of its members. We can understand, through Gordon, what it means to be a Minuteman.

Searching for His Place

When Gordon and I first met in April 2006, it was his first time participating in a patrol operation with the Minutemen, and throughout the month he revealed feelings of exclusion and frustration.

To participate, he drove for two days all the way from his home in Ohio in a red Ford sedan. At the Minutemen camp the car was dwarfed by the set of Jeeps and stations wagons that surrounded it.

Gordon purchased a brand-new tent, which he told me had set him back nearly $150. It was his first time camping since his days as a Boy Scout, and he hated it. Each morning Gordon woke up complaining about how uncomfortable it was and about how he was sick of all the dust that constantly blew all over his clothes. Often he would jealously point out Minutemen who had come with RVs and claim that next time he was going to fly down instead of driving all the way from Ohio, and rent himself an RV as well.

Like many volunteers, Gordon first heard about the Minutemen through the Internet. Prior to joining, he had been a frequent listener to what he called conservative radio and read reports of conservative news outlets. It was while reading the website of one of these that he came across an advertisement for the Minutemen.

After attending a Minutemen recruitment meeting in Cleveland, Gordon participated in the picketing of a bank that was accused of giving loans to "illegals." When he tells me the story of the picket, he focuses on the second day of the protest. "Some folks from the university, a labor group, you know, a bunch of socialists, they started a counterprotest. Well, this fight broke out. They brought in some ringers, they wanted to start a fight, and they attacked this one guy who was sixty-five. But let me tell you, they messed with the wrong guy, he was a Minuteman, he was an ex-Marine, and he was also a black belt in karate."

In his account of the story, Gordon not only focuses on the fight but also underscores the warriorlike traits of the Minuteman, traits which he himself did not possess, and which he worried made him unfit to be a Minuteman. "The guy, he kind of liked me, and he says to me, 'Have you ever gone down on a patrol?' And I had heard about them and I says to him, 'I don't know if I'm up to it,' and he was basically like, 'We'd love to have you come down.'"

Gordon explains that during the first trip he made to the border, he didn't even know what the term "muster" meant, learning only afterward that it was military parlance for a gathering of troops. He also says that when he went out on patrol for the first time he had a "very memorable experience." This was in part because of the anxiety he says he felt "the first time I sat down on the chair in the middle of night, in the middle the desert, not knowing what was going to come at me." But beyond this, Gordon tells me it was memorable because he was able to witness illegal immigrants passing nearby to where he was posted. "It was really neat, I had just been taught how to use the infrared camera by one of the guys I was with, and I spotted a group of them. They even let me call it in myself to command center." Gordon gives a chuckle, "And then, it was amazing, Border Patrol came by with the Black Hawk helicopter. They had the lights flashing and they were hovering right near us. I had never seen a Black Hawk before in person like that, and it really put a chill in me, it was quite an experience."

When most members reflect on their first experience going on patrol, they often make sense of it by drawing comparisons to their time in the military. Like Gordon, they also express anxiety, but, unlike him, they connect their anxiety to their previous life experiences in the military. Take, for example, Brian, a Vietnam War veteran. Brian tells me that the first time he was on patrol he heard some noises that his partner told him might be illegals. Brian recalls being frightened. It was the kind of fear that took him back to the jungles of Vietnam. "I puckered up," he testifies. "You know, like when your ass cheeks close up 'cause you're all scared? It was just like in 'Nam when you'd get spooked Charlie was nearby." Or consider Steve's reflections on his first time on patrol: "I just kept looking at all those shooting stars light up the sky and remembering the flares in Vietnam. Man, it really took me back."

As is common procedure, new members of the Minutemen are placed along with experienced volunteers on their first patrol. Gordon says he received a lot of "training" from the two members he was partnered with, whom he describes as "tough guys; one used to be a colonel in the air force, the other was a marine." As Gordon retells this experience, he talks about the two other volunteers with awe and reverence, which, at the same time that it communicated respect and praise, also communicated that he himself lacked what they had. Gordon says that the colonel and marine gave him "the insights I needed to know about how to patrol, about how it all worked." Among the things Gordon says he was taught was "how important it was to keep quiet. . . . They had to keep disciplining me that first time until I got it into my head that we were on stealth mode. . . . By now it's second nature."

In Gordon's recounting of his initial experience on patrol, which extended over thirty minutes, he never once talked about the colonel's or marine's beliefs about illegal immigrants. That's not what made them colonels or marines, and that's not what made them the kind of men Gordon wanted to be—the kind of men he was in the process of trying to become.

Gordon says that when he first went out on patrol, most people on the line were referred to by nicknames, and at one point the two people who were training him explained, "'If you want to be serious about patrolling, you need to get yourself a handle.'" Back at camp, he thought about what handle to take on. He says that other Minutemen used the names they had while they were in the service, and since he didn't serve, he had to come up with one. Gordon says people told him that the handle should express something about who he is, either in terms of where he is from or what hobbies he enjoys. After giving it some thought, he chose the name "Dune" based on the title of his favorite book.

Gordon's acquisition of a handle represented the start of a transformation in his identity. It was a transformation not in his ideology, but in what Erving Goffman calls his "presentation of self."[2]

In Goffman's dramaturgical approach to social interaction, identities are achieved and maintained through performances. Like actors on the stage in a theater, people perform a role and follow a script in everyday life. Different identities follow different kinds of scripts and require different kinds of performances. From this perspective, identity is not simply something people *have* but rather something people *do*.

For Goffman, an important feature of the performance of an identity comes from the "identity kit," which includes clothing and related accessories that help signify to others who we are. Gordon's acquisition of a handle represented the beginning of his acquisition of a new identity kit—that of a solider—through which he is able to perform the role of a Minuteman. It is a performance that also includes gaining a new way of managing his body.

In Bourdieu's definition, an important part of the habitus has to do with how people carry themselves. This refers to physical appearance, but also to how people use their bodies when doing things. In these ways the habitus, Bourdieu says, is embodied. Our acquired dispositions and knowledge shape our bodies, and the habitus makes itself known first and foremost not through the mind, but through the body. In the Minutemen camp, the military men embody a military habitus, and it manifests itself in disparate ways, from the way they walk, to the way they know how to track footprints in the desert, to the way they know how to reload a gun. Gordon arrived at the Minuteman camp with a different kind of habitus.

A Man without a Place

Gordon made a great effort to be involved at the camp. When he first introduced himself to me, he told me that he held the position of camp coordinator and that he was responsible for helping out around camp and making sure people had everything they needed. This, it turned out, was a position he had volunteered for. And the position that he volunteered for was, in the organizational structure of the Minutemen camp, a highly feminine one.

Officially it was Susan who held the position of taking care of the camp, from making sure there was fresh coffee, to cleaning up the trash, to monitoring people's pets while they went out on patrol. Gordon's participation in these activities was a departure from what most men were expected to do, but it was the only thing, at that point, that Gordon was both allowed to do and capable of doing. And he took his job as coordinator very seriously. Rather than talking about it in a way that indicated it was "women's work," he told me that he saw the tasks as important contributions.

But in the Minutemen camp these were not the types of things men did—not the kind of men the camp glorified. In the Minutemen camp there was a place for women to be women and men to be men, but no place for anything in between. There was no place for Gordon to be Gordon.

One morning, about two weeks into the operation, as Gordon and I were sharing a coffee outside our tents, he informed me that he was very upset at the way he was being treated at camp. He told me that the other day, while he was sitting with some members of the scouting team as they were discussing patrolling strategies, they treated him very disrespectfully. "You know, they're former marines and what not, they feel like they are the big shots around here. They walk around with their guns, and they have their little clique. And they don't care for what I had to say."

The group of people Gordon was referring to are longtime members of the organization who have taken up primary roles in the tactical organization of patrol operations. Like most Minutemen, they are former members of the United States military, and, for the most part, they have the most military experience of all the volunteers in the camp.

Gordon did not fit in with the marines. They were disrespectful, and Gordon couldn't take it anymore. "I have a bunch of ideas about how they are running the operations, ways to make it better, more organized. But they just ignored me. And then at one point, in front of everyone, Norm makes fun of me, I mean right there in front of everyone. . . . I was telling them that I would like to volunteer to help out, you know with the scouting and strategizing. And Norm says that I can help out by cleaning around camp."

Gordon continued, explaining why he thought they were not being more respectful of his suggestions, "It might have something to do with the fact that I didn't serve in Vietnam, you know, I think they think that that doesn't give me any right to say anything. But you know that's not how you run an organization. I mean I have a lot of knowledge and experience about how to run things, but they don't want to listen. I might not know a lot about guns or the military, but I do know how to work with people, and I have a lot of good ideas." The problem, for Gordon, was that the skills he had were managerial skills, not soldiering skills, not the skills that made one a Minuteman. And he started to understand this. On patrol he saw the other volunteers using handheld radios and night-vision goggles; at the camp he heard them talking military strategy and military experience. Frustrated, he repeatedly complained to me that he wished someone at the camp would teach a class on how to use radios, or how to properly use firearms: "You know, they should take some time, one of the military guys, and run a couple classes. They could do something like once a week for us guys who don't have these skills."

If there is someone who had the skills that makes one a Minuteman, it is Blowfish. Now in his late sixties, Blowfish admits he is not in the same physical shape as he used to be. Patting his large belly, he joked, "I didn't always have this." But Blowfish doesn't need to hide his belly—he doesn't even need to dress in camouflage, which he never does. Instead, he wears jeans and a solid-colored t-shirt. But it doesn't matter. Unlike the others—not just Gordon, but everyone else—Blowfish had accumulated so much respect by way of his past that his status as a respected soldier doesn't even need to be stressed. Indeed, it is the lack of outward effort made to convey that he is a soldier—a crafted performance itself—that gave off the powerful impression that not only was Blowfish a soldier, he was one in ways that the other men were not.

Blowfish climbed the ranks in the army, making it to the elite Special Forces of the United States military. He didn't talk very much about what that entailed, and the secrecy provided him with yet more legitimacy. But while Blowfish didn't talk much about his experiences, others did.

They talked about the grueling qualification courses Blowfish had to complete to become a Green Beret. They talked about the obstacle courses he must have been through, the 20-mile hikes in the middle of the desert while carrying 100-pound loads on his shoulders. They talked about how he had to go through training to prepare himself, not just for battle, but for capture. "I'll put my money they beat him," a volunteer told me. "That's right, they tortured him, that's how they prepare those Special Ops people for the chance that they might be captured." Another volunteer remarked, "You put this guy in the middle of nowhere and he'll survive. That's what they trained him for. He'll live on dirt and grass if he has to."

The respect and admiration given to Blowfish, reflected not just by the other volunteers' comments but by the fact that he held the position of head of all the line leaders, points to the value placed in the Minutemen camp on military experience and military skills, something that Gordon, at that point, lacked. Gordon had skills: managerial skills. But unlike Blowfish's skills, they were not easily translatable into the cultural capital of masculinity and soldiering. Unlike Blowfish, whose biography was a source of respect, Gordon's own background served as a barrier to be overcome. It is not an ideology that he had to overcome but a way of being in the world. What Gordon lacked when he first joined the group were not a set of beliefs but a set of dispositions.

Gordon and His Guns

When Gordon and I met again in October 2006, more than half a year since he had started volunteering with the Minutemen, there were numerous changes to his identity kit. Unlike the first time I met him, Gordon was now, like most members, dressed in military attire. He still had his Ford and his tent, both now well weathered by their time in Arizona. I also noticed that he had put bumper stickers on his car indicating that he was a supporter of Tom Tancredo, and another explaining to people in not so polite words that he was against illegal immigration.

Tancredo, a Republican congressman from Colorado, is known for his hard-line views against illegal immigration, which include deportation of all those currently residing in the United States illegally as well as construction of a fence along the entire border. Among Minutemen he was a political hero. I asked Gordon about the sticker, and he told me that he had obtained it from one of the other Minutemen. He then told me that he had also acquired a gun.

"When I first came down here, I had no idea about what was actually going on down here. I seen all these old grannies with their binoculars on the news, but then I came here and got the real deal, I got to realize just how dangerous it is down here. I got to understand that it's a war zone down here." "That," Gordon emphatically added, "is when I decided that I would also start taking my gun with me."

Later that month, Norm and I decided to go to an outdoor firing range located about thirty minutes away from the camp. We had been talking about it for a few days, and Gordon, who overheard us, was excited about the prospect of joining in.

Norm is in his late forties and a private business owner. He was well respected in the organization and was involved in most of the tactical decisions made regarding patrol operations. He was a member of the Minutemen's Search and Rescue Team, an elite unit within the organization with special privileges and responsibilities. Along with running his business, Norm was also a National Rifle Association (NRA) licensed gun instructor and ran workshops a few times a year where he taught people basic weaponry skills. Even though, like Gordon, he was from Ohio, the two did not have a warm relationship.

When Gordon first heard that I was scheduling a time to go to the firing range with Norm, he informed me that he really wanted to learn a lot more about how to use guns. He said that he felt like he doesn't know enough and needed to get more knowledge. Echoing Goffman's ideas about identity as a performance, Gordon said to me, "If you encounter a smuggler on patrol, well, you at least need to *look* like you know what are doing!" In this instance, because I lacked the kind of status the marines had, I served as an audience to which Gordon could be self-deprecating in a way that he could not be in front of the marines.

Gordon told me that in previous operations he had spoken to Norm about his desire to learn more about guns, and that the two of them had made plans to meet in Ohio, but these never came to fruition. I told Gordon that I would be very glad for him to come with us to the firing range, and once I arranged a time with Norm, I informed Gordon about it. Gordon was very excited about the prospect. When the time came I met Norm at his Jeep, climbed into the passenger seat, and buckled in, and before I knew it Norm started to drive off, leaving Gordon behind waiting at his tent. As he started to drive I asked him if Gordon was coming with us, and the only response I got was a foot pressed down further on the gas pedal.

About half an hour after Norm and I got to the firing range, Gordon arrived by himself. While Norm was explaining safety measures to me, Gordon walked past us, visibly discontented, and took aim at a firing station nearby. As Norm instructed me on the proper positioning of my elbow, Gordon started firing off rounds from an enormous revolver he had holstered on his hip. The size of the gun made Gordon's motions, even to my untrained eye, look awkwardly novice. He put the gun in his side holster and removed it in a flash, as if reenacting a scene from one of his favorite Hollywood Westerns. Gordon's over-the-top performance did not go unnoticed by Norm, who turned to me and, shaking his head, noted that "There are even some Minutemen who could use some education on guns."

A few days after the experience at the firing range I asked Gordon if I could go on patrol with him, and he excitedly agreed, adding that he would be glad to "show me how its done."

When we gathered at 4 p.m., along with the twenty other volunteers who were going out on patrol, for the mandatory prepatrol briefing, I discovered another accoutrement Gordon had added to his identity kit: a cigar. Throughout the briefing, as Mike and John, who were serving as the line leaders for the shift, went over the logistics, Gordon struck a cool pose, chomping on an unlit cigar and appearing to be indifferent to what was being said.

There were a total of eight posts going on patrol in the evening's swing shift. At the end of the briefing Gordon and I received our large stadium light, which was to be turned on when illegal immigrants are spotted, as well as a radio that was connected to the main communications center located at the ranch. Along with this main communications line, some members had a second radio, a personal one known as a "peanut" for its diminutive size. This radio line was to be used, sparsely, for communications unrelated to operations. Gordon had purchased a peanut for himself and offered me control over it. He helped me clip it to my belt and set up the earpiece, and he gave me a quick run-through of the activation system.

Gordon and I were stationed on the "Cuervo Grande" or "Large Raven" patrol line, designated in reference to the similarly named windy dirt road that veers off the main highway that connects Arizona with Mexico. When we were directed to our line post, Gordon made a great effort to park his car as close as he could to a large mesquite tree. As he struggled to maneuver his car in the damp mud, cigar still in mouth, he explained the reason for his efforts: "This way the tree will give us cover so that they don't see the car. I've got camouflage netting in the trunk that we'll put over it too, but this way it'll be fully out of sight."

While Gordon kept working on positioning his car ever closer to the mesquite tree, he instructed me to get out of the car and scout the area for the best location to set up our lawn chairs. I walked aimlessly back and forth along the 50-foot radius that I was told bounded our post, waiting for Gordon to get out of the car. He walked over to me and said that a good spot offered two things: it must be concealed, and it must offer a good view of the desert. I walked around, unable to determine any differences in the unmarked landscape that would qualify for either of these. There was a large bush jutting out of the earth, and I threw down my lawn chair and said, "How's that?" He told me I had the right idea, except that I placed the chair facing northward, that is, away from the border. "If they're coming, they're going to be coming from in front of us," Gordon scolded me, pointing in the direction of Mexico in a fatherly way.

He scanned the terrain for a few moments. "It's always important," he told me, "to walk around the area while there is still light. It's important to know the terrain, know what's around you, get a good reading of your bearings. Because in a few hours its going get real dark out here and you can't see what's two feet in front of you." After I walked around our post a few times with Gordon, being told of particular divots and cacti to be mindful of, he told me he had found a good spot to set up our chairs. "You see this, Harel, you see this little path in the desert, you see these footprints, this is where they will be coming from." As he explained his choice to me, pointing out a narrow path with traces of shoeprints in it, as well as two empty water jugs with Spanish writing on them, Mike and John drove by and stopped at our post.

Mike and John both got out of their car and, after a bit of cordial exchanges, told Gordon that he should try to park his car at a different spot because he was too far in the road. They drove off. Gordon was incensed.

"Did you see that Harel? Did you see how they said that? They didn't have to say that. Like there is really something wrong with where I put the car. He wants me to move it another two inches. See they just like to play boss-man and give everyone orders. They just like to be in control, that's all it is. Why make me look bad like that?" I asked Gordon why he thought they were acting like that, and he continued his tirade, "See the way it works around here is that you have these guys with big egos. Mike thinks he knows better than everyone else, and he likes to go around and tell people what to do, but he doesn't want to hear any suggestions." Suddenly Gordon froze, "Is that peanut on?" He grabbed the radio that was clipped to my belt. A green light was flashing. "Oh lord," he said. "I think you had the talk function on, I think they just overheard all of that."

Gordon was distressed. I was shaking. I tried to reassure myself as well as Gordon, offering that they hadn't heard anything, and that even if they had, he didn't say anything that bad. Gordon took hold of the radio. A call came in. "Yup, it was on, we heard everything you said, Gordon." Another call came in, "Oh, oh Gordon, you're in trouble." His face was filled with anxiety; he looked as if he was trying to decide whether to say something or to keep quiet. I began to assault him with a wave of apologies. Then he spoke into the radio and in a joking tone said, "That's right, it's true, you know those former marines, coming out here with their chests all puffed out." A few more calls came in joking about the event. Neither Mike nor John responded.

Gordon's response to Mike and John was the first time since I met him that he had asserted some agency. Indeed, much as this was a moment of embarrassment for Gordon, he took it as an opportunity to embarrass Mike and John and criticize the "puffy-chested" masculinity that was being promoted at the camp. And Gordon was not the only one to criticize these men. The camp was a place where not only did people like Gordon get disciplined, but also people like Mike and John. The camp was at once a concerted manifestation of a masculine and soldierly way of being, a way of being that was imported from the outside world and previous life experiences, but also a producer of that way of being. And it was not only Gordon who had to adjust. In his response on the radio, he indicated an element of contestation to the hegemonic masculinity being promoted by the group. But at the same time that he criticized it, he slowly came to embody it.

Finding His Place

In October 2007, nearly two years into his tenure with the Minutemen, Gordon arrives at camp with a Harley Davidson motorcycle and a sport-utility vehicle. He has also purchased an expensive CB radio and taken a course back in Ohio on how to use it. These investments represented a significant share of his fixed income.

Along with his new motorcycle and car, Gordon also dresses differently from before, now wearing full military fatigues, including high ankle boots. At least outwardly, he has changed in dramatic ways. Beyond the clothing, there is a stark difference in the way he carries himself, walking around the camp self-confidently and speaking to people in an authoritative tone.

Gordon has also become one of the most involved members at the camp. Except, unlike when I first met him, his involvement now comes strictly in the form of going out on patrols. And it is not just any patrols; Gordon has become one of the more active participants in the grave-yard shifts. While these shifts have the greatest likelihood of encounters with illegal immigrants, the significant difference between them and the other shifts is not so much in terms of the practical impact they have on stopping illegal immigrants, but rather the symbolic weight they carry in defining oneself as a heroic soldier. And Gordon knows this. We may think that he goes out on these overnight patrols because he wants to catch more Mexicans, and that is not necessarily untrue. But if Gordon wants to catch Mexicans, it is not for the simple reason of enforcing im-migration laws or stopping Mexicans from coming into his community; it is to be able to gain acceptance with the Minutemen. As Gordon puts it to me when I ask him about his going on overnight patrols on five consecutive nights in October 2007, "I want to prove myself."

For Gordon, the Minutemen camp holds the appeal of finding mean-ing and self-worth. For him, gaining acceptance from the marines is a way of gaining validation of his masculinity. But not everyone has that experience. There are a good number of volunteers who come to the camp in search of meaning, only to find alienation. And unlike Gordon, they don't struggle to gain acceptance; they don't find the approval of the military men appealing or meaningful. There are a number of people who come to the camp and leave.

They are people like Terry and Janice, a retired couple from Minne-sota. When Terry and Janice made too much noise on the patrol line, Blowfish let them know such behavior was unacceptable. And when Terry and Janice laughed about it, Blowfish told them they had to either "shape up" or leave. They decided to leave. "Hey, I am not in the army here," Terry explained to me as he packed his bags, "I am just a vol-unteer." But what lures men like Gordon to the Minutemen camp is precisely the fact this is a place where they can be more than "just a vol-unteer"; they can be soldiers. They can be men. As a volunteer explained to me, those who could not deal with Blowfish were not men. "If people complained about how mean he was to them, as far as I am concerned, they were pussies and they should have been given a pacifier and had their asses sent home to mommy."

Gordon purchased his Harley because of Jolene. It was also partially because of her that he was able to achieve his newfound status in the camp.

Jolene is in her late fifties. She is skinny and has gray hair that still has traces of her former blond. You can tell she was quite good-looking back in the day, and in the context of the camp, surrounded by women who are mostly much older and have long stopped taking care of their appearance or engaging in flirtatious behavior, Jolene draws a lot of the men's attention.

Jolene does a lot of things that would give the impression that she is not a "feminine" woman. Up until four years ago she was a corrections officer. When she retired she sold her home and decided to spend her time traveling across the country in a motor home. She rides a Harley Davidson. She patrols the border. But she does these things with an air of refinement.

In the morning she takes her two poodles around the camp for a walk. In the afternoon she sweeps up the "welcome" mat in front of her motor home—a motor home she has named Charlie. At night she sits on a leather folding chair in front of Charlie and sips wine out of a metallic glass. But for Jolene, who is no longer married, no longer works, and no longer owns a home, the camp is not just a place separate from her everyday life, it *is* her everyday life. When she comes down to the border, she doesn't just bring her Minutemen gear, she brings her entire life. And what you feel most powerfully watching Jolene as she lives out her life, as you see everything that she owns spread out inside Charlie, is a sense of loneliness; she drinks her wine alone; she occupies only one of the two queen-sized beds in the motor home; Charlie is the only man in her life. But then came Gordon.

Jolene and Gordon began going out on patrols together. At first they did it sporadically; then they did it habitually. Then they started spending time at the camp together, eating meals together, going for walks and drives together. And although he never announced it outright to the others, Gordon also didn't shy away from making it known that Jolene had taken to him. It was within the confines of this masculine space that a woman was the one who was able to give Gordon the ultimate affirmation of his masculinity. It was by virtue of being with her, and being seen with her, that he was conferred some of his status as a man.

In the middle of the month, as I am sitting and eating in the dining area with Dale, one of the directors of the organization, Gordon walks by and Dale calls him over. Dale tells Gordon that he has heard great things about him from other people in the camp, and that he wants to ask him to consider joining the Search and Rescue Team. Gordon indicates that he is very flattered by the offer but says that he is worried that his lack of military training might not qualify him. Dale explains that not everyone in the unit has military experience, and that other members will train him. Throughout the conversation Gordon is very serious and keeps an earnest demeanor that belies the excitement he later reveals to me. Gordon takes me to the side and tells me about the "promotion" he has been offered. He tells me that apart from being asked to join the Search and Rescue Team, he has also been asked to serve as a line leader, and Dale has invited him to his house to have dinner. "Dale is from the business world, you see," Gordon explains to me. "He used to work on Michigan Avenue in Chicago, and that's how they do it, when they want you on board, when they want to move you up to a higher position, they wine and dine you."

Indeed, I had known that many of the high-ranking members of the Minutemen had often been invited to Dale's home, the invitation serving as a ritual to signify what sociologists often refer to as "crossing an organizational boundary," rites of passage that signify to the person that they have gained full membership.[3]

A few days later Gordon tells me that he has made some suggestions about how to organize the patrols and that they have been taken up. Up to that point, patrol assignments were named based on the actual given name of the location; for example, patrols on Cuervo Grande were called "Cuervo Grande. Gordon's suggestion was to come up with pseudonyms for the patrol assignments, so that they will not be known to the coyotes, who are supposedly listening in on the radio, which operates on a public frequency. "You don't tell your enemy where you are going to be," Gordon proudly clarifies to me. "It's simple, don't say 'Cuervo Grande' if that is where we are going to be; give it another name."

The next day when I gather along with others in preparation to patrol Cuervo Grande, the line leader instructs us that it has been renamed "Dune."

Fighting for His Place

Gordon thinks of himself as a fighter. Now in his late sixties, he lives close to where he grew up, in a small town in suburban Ohio, just outside

Toledo. He has reddish skin, a square, wrinkled face, and dimples, and he blushes easily. He is a bit shorter than average height, and even though he is not that small he seems to think he is, being very self-conscious of his size and often referring to himself as "not a big guy." But what Gordon thinks he lacks in size he says he makes up for in heart. "I'm kind of like, 'I don't care if you do whoop my ass, I'm still gonna fight.'"

Gordon's repeated assertion of his status as a fighter connects to a larger claim about himself as a masculine man. But these claims are embedded within another story, a story of fear and a damaged masculinity; a masculinity that he has lost and wants to reclaim.

As Gordon tells it, the story of his life is one of missed opportunities. He was previously the assistant manager of a grocery store that had a conjoined pharmacy. Proudly, he tells me that he was in charge of organizing all the store's operations and that he had over twenty people working under him. A few years into managing this store, he was approached by a close friend with an offer to start a sandwich business together; Gordon says he was excited about the prospect of working on his own and was set to leave his job until the owner of the grocery store convinced him otherwise. Gordon, who is constantly worried about being duped, and often thinks that he is, says that when he thinks back on it, he is suspicious of the motives behind his boss's behavior toward him: "You see Harel, the guy knew I was a really good worker, and that I was really important to his business. So he tells me all this stuff about how I won't make any money with the sandwich business but really he was doing it out of self-interest; he didn't care what was good for me. I just wasn't smart enough to realize it at the time. And you know what, sure as heck that friend of mine went on to make big money."

Gordon is an inquisitive person. He spends a great deal of his free time at the Minutemen campground reading magazines such as *Popular Mechanics* and *Science*. He says that many times while stimulated by these magazines he has come up with a number of great ideas for inventions, but he has never pursued them: "Hell Harel," he testifies to me, "I have had so many lost opportunities. . . . My life is just a number of lost opportunities, one after the other."

Along with missed opportunities, a second theme running through Gordon's interpretation of his past is being mistreated by women. On numerous occasions he would ask me questions regarding my own relations with women as an occasion to introduce his own past experiences.

Gordon was twice divorced. In his early twenties he married his high school sweetheart. In high school he was a wrestling champion, and back then, he adds, he was considered quite good-looking. "You know, I was buff and all then, not like I am now."

He speaks about the excitement he felt when he was a senior in high school and one of the prettiest girls asked him to the prom. The two ended up getting married, and it lasted over ten years until she began cheating on him. "And you know what the worst part of it was?" Gordon says. "She did it a lot of times, and she didn't hide it, she would tell me about men she would be seeing." Finally he divorced her to save his own "self-respect," even though "she ended up receiving a lot of my money."

Gordon's second marriage was to an alcoholic and lasted only four years. When he retells troubling stories about his second wife, he does so more with embarrassment than a sense of anger toward her. "At first I thought she just liked to drink a little bit, but after a while I realized she had a serious problem. We would be having lunch, and even before we finish ordering she would already have drank two glasses of wine. . . . And then she would always make scenes in public when she was drunk. She would start yelling at me, cursing me in front of all these people. I would be so ashamed. And you know Harel, I'm just not the confrontational type, I don't yell, so you know we would be sitting there at this nice restaurant and she would be screaming at me and I would just sit there and take it."

The past, while a chronicle of mistreatment and being taken advantage of, was also a refuge for Gordon. While adulthood was marred by failures, Gordon often retold stories of a happy and adventurous youth—of how, for instance, when he was a young teenager he would spend his summers in Arkansas working for his uncle, a "fruit peddler," who sold produce in what Gordon described as "poor black communities that were not well serviced." "Those summers are some of my fondest memories," he would mourn, "I would go back up to Ohio with a bag full of firecrackers and sell them to some of the kids in the neighborhood—you know they were illegal at the time in Ohio, but you could get them for cheap down in Arkansas. At first I just bought them for fun, for myself, but then when I got back home all the other kids were jealous and they wanted some, so I started selling them. It wasn't that much money I made, you know, just something extra to keep in my pocket for the arcade or what not. But it was really neat, you know, I was the cool kid and everyone in the neighborhood was excited whenever I came back from Arkansas."

Gordon currently lives on one side of a two-family home located on a long residential street. Although he and his neighbors have separate entrances, their homes are connected to each other and they share a porch. His neighbors are a middle-aged couple with two teenage children. Although they live in close proximity to each other, Gordon rarely interacts with his neighbors. What interaction there is usually happens between Gordon and the neighbors' kids while he is mowing the lawn and they are out playing in the front yard.

There is very little street life in Gordon's neighborhood. The only traffic comes either from people driving to and from work or from the occasional neighborhood child riding a bicycle. It's the kind of street you wouldn't enter unless you lived on it or were visiting someone who did. Gordon himself rarely has visitors. It's not that he's unfriendly or that he likes to keep to himself. In fact, it's the opposite. He is both a very friendly person and eager to talk with people, given the opportunity. The problem is that aren't very many opportunities.

The majority of Gordon's everyday interactions take place at the grocery store or the post office. In search of a good chat, he's recently been spending more and more time at the local car dealership, where he's developed a friendly rapport with the dealer who sold him his SUV. The highlight of Gordon's week comes on Saturdays when he makes a forty-five-minute drive to visit his daughter and watch his nephew play Little League baseball.

When the suburbs where Gordon lives were first established, they were segregated enclaves of white America. They were the places where middle- and working-class people went after commuting to the city for work—the kinds of commute Gordon used to make.. But times have changed. The borders have been broken, and the "enemy" has penetrated the walls that once kept him at bay. The enemy is now living inside what was once a symbolic and spatial haven for people like Gordon.

"There have been a lot of changes," he tells me. "So many Hispanics have moved in. You know there was one place where I used to live about fifteen minutes from where I am now, and I had to leave. I was evicted from my own home. I was actually ran out of my home because of illegals."

The changes that have brought the enemy closer include the shift from an economy organized around manufacturing to one based on the service sector. It is an economy that mobilizes the law to produce an army of cheap, low-skilled labor, an economy where job creation entails the creation of a demand for such people. The changes include a change from policies organized around maintaining racially segregated spaces to increasingly diverse ones, from a politics of segregation to a politics of integration. They are changes that have seen the demographics of Gordon's community change dramatically, most poignantly with regard to the number of Hispanics. According to census figures, the Latino population in Ohio has increased by 63 percent since 2000 and nearly tripled since 1980. The county where Gordon lives has seen the greatest change.[4] They are changes that he is having a difficult time adjusting to.

For Gordon, the presence of this new population is understood, unequivocally, as an eviction—their arrival comes at the cost of his own dignity. He understands these newcomers as an invading army, whose very presence entails the loss of his own place in the world.

In 2008, Gordon decided to move. I ask him for more details about why he moved, and he tells me, "I was surrounded by people speaking Spanish, people who don't like me because I am this white guy. It just wasn't comfortable to be there anymore, it's not a place for white people, not a place for English speakers. . . . It started out a nice neighborhood and we never had a police call ever, and then the illegals came. . . . Little by little things started happening. They were stealing my mail. There was fighting going on all the time, drunken fighting. I caught the neighbors stealing my newspaper—they called it 'borrowing'—the kids were destructive, tearing down my evergreens, they were throwing rocks at the building, I couldn't park my car outside. . . . It was a constant aggravation. . . . Finally I decided I had too much and I moved out."

When Gordon first arrived at the Minutemen camp, he arrived without the same habitus as the other men, but like them, he arrived with a sense that he had no purpose and place in contemporary America. Like them, he arrived in southern Arizona not in search of an ideology, not in support of a government policy, but in search of a place to belong, a place to call home. But unlike the others, Gordon had to learn to take on a way of being that fits with this place.

Gordon's pilgrimage to the border made him a new person, not in the sense that he learned a new ideology, but in the sense that he learned a new way of carrying himself in the world—a way of carrying himself that he carried from Arizona all the way back to Ohio.

After graduating from high school Gordon refused to join the army. He tells me that he didn't really believe in the Vietnam War because he thought soldiers were getting sent to be killed for no good reason. He remembers a very tense moment when he told his father that he wasn't going to serve in the military if they called him to enlist. "I looked him square in the eyes and I said to him, Dad, I don't mean to embarrass you, but they are going to have to come get me with guns."

Now Gordon was out to get other people with guns.

When I met with him at the end of 2008 at his home in Ohio, he explained to me that for the past month he had taken it on himself to start patrolling a park near his home. "There is this nice little park, with picnic tables and lots of open space, and the Mexicans, they always go there early in the day and take it over. You know, they sit there and intimidate everyone so no one else can use it. Well, I started going there real early in the morning, at around 5 a.m., and I put on my Border Patrol hat, my Minuteman shirt, my army pants, and I wear my gun, and I walk around the park. You know, I intimidate them right back. This is America, it's my country, you know, I'm not going to let them intimidate me."

ANDREA DYLEWSKI

CHAPTER 4

Scenes from the Border

IIIIIIIIIIIIIIIIIIIIIIIIIIIIIIIIIIIIIIIII

The Border as a Place to Suffer

Tom, Roger, and I have not moved for nearly three hours. I can't take it anymore. I'm freezing. I'm restless. I look over to see if I can read similar signs of exasperation on Tom's or Roger's face. Roger is asleep. His seventy-year-old body is hunched over the lawn chair. Tom, in his sixties, is two feet away, two feet too far for me to be able to see him. In the desert, nights are truly pitch black. But Tom has a bad cold and I know he's awake because I can hear him sniffling.

I want to ask if I can get up and walk around a bit. But the sun has set long ago and we are now on "stealth" mode. Not only are you not supposed to move about, but talking is to be kept to a minimum—only to things that mattered, only to things pertaining to the operation. Nighttime is when José makes his move, and it's imperative the enemy doesn't know we're waiting.

One of the desert's secrets is its frigid nights. The overwhelming daytime heat is anticipated, but not the nighttime cold. No more than two hours after the sun goes down, the temperature drops by half. It is a shock to the system. The barren landscape magnifies this. Just as during the daytime there is no cover for the sun's rays, during the night unchecked winds slam into your body. And when you're not allowed to move, the cold feels that much colder.

Like most Minutemen, Tom and Roger learned about the cold the hard way. A couple of years back they arrived at their first border patrol poorly equipped. Sure, they had read the informational handouts new recruits were given outlining what to bring and had e-mail exchanges with veteran members about what to expect. Sure, they had followed the advice they were given. They brought their military fatigues, camping gear, handheld radios, and handguns. What they didn't bring was a blanket. By now, themselves veterans of patrolling the border, they have come prepared for battle. They wear jackets, gloves, and hats. A blanket is draped over each of them.

Tom and Roger were both in the air force. Roger dropped bombs over Korea; Tom, over Vietnam. In their physical appearance, the ten-year age difference comes across as if it were much greater. Apart from a few wrinkles, Tom has well-maintained features. He has a sturdy walk to go along with sturdy hands. Roger, on the other hand, has a droopy face. He walks hunched over and with a limp. Their physical features and ways of carrying themselves reveal not only an age difference, but also a class difference.

Tom is an upper-middle-class professional. He is clean-cut and wears delicate glasses. He walks around camp in trousers and a neatly tucked button-down shirt. Now retired, Roger used to work at a car fleet company. He lets his hair go where it wants. The hair on his head is a bushy mess, and gray hairs grow out of his ears and on his nose. He wears an oversized flannel shirt and sweatpants. While Tom owns a sophisticated new minivan; Roger tows a boxy old camper behind a beat-up station wagon. While Tom has a serious demeanor and rarely cracks a smile, Roger has childish sensibilities, often talking in funny voices and pulling pranks around the camp. He wakes up in the morning and walks up to volunteers inquiring, "Donde está la cantina?"

But there is much this odd couple has in common. For one, they both think America is "going to shit." And it is there, in the middle of the massive Arizona desert, sitting on lawn chairs, covered in blankets, that they feel they are doing something about it.

Tom and Roger are very pleased as we receive our patrol assignment at 4:00 in the afternoon. They like the Alpha line. Tom says it could have been better, he prefers the Bravo line. There's more "action" over there. But "the Alpha is better than some of the others." They're also excited I'm coming with them. They go out of their way to make sure we get a "good spot" on the line. They want to make sure that I get to see some "action."

Blowfish tells everyone gathered for the prepatrol briefing to keep their eyes peeled. The previous night's shift reported a number of sightings. "They're crossing, boys, they're crossing," he says with his eyes affixed to the clipboard in his hand, which has the specific post assignments. I can't tell if his comment is meant as a directive or a cheer. Probably both. And it seems that that's how the volunteers take it, smiling at the same time as they check to make sure they have all their gear ready.

Before the briefing, Tom approached Blowfish to try to see if he could ensure we would be placed at a hot spot on the line. Tom says it makes a big difference where you are on the line. Some posts are believed to have more action because they have more strategic locations. He doesn't want to be put on a "boring one." When he approaches Blowfish he does so cautiously. Blowfish runs a tight ship, and he won't be induced into anything he doesn't think is good for the operation. The two exchange a few words. Blowfish scans the clipboard in his hand. His motions suggest he will see what he can do.

Blowfish is set to announce the assignments. Everyone is excited. Throughout the previous ten-minute briefing, when Blowfish went through the various rules and regulations, you sensed you were around a group of teenage kids at a swimming pool, biting their lip while the adult went through a spiel that everyone, while pretending to care, didn't want to hear.

Tom shoots me a wink and a smile. Blowfish put us at a good spot. Not only that, he gave us one of the highly sought after night-vision scopes. Tom has one of his own. Normally you're supposed to only have one per post, but Tom doesn't speak up to say so. "It can't hurt to have another," he says to me under his breath. Along with the night-vision scope, we are given the standard equipment that everyone gets: a stadium-size flashlight and a radio. Things are looking good.

The convoy of pickup trucks and SUVs line up in order of their position on the line. Blowfish is up front. He is the shepherd of the pilgrimage. Tom, Roger, and I are all in Tom's minivan. It still has that new car smell. But it's a total mess from his days of camping out. Clothes and camping gear are strewn around. I am lying on the floor behind folded-down seats. Tom has taken to sleeping in his van the past few nights because it's too cold to be in a tent.

It's a thirty-minute drive on paved road from the campground to the Alpha line. From there it's another thirty on dirt. We come up to a small wooden stick with a pink ribbon on its end. Tom says this must be our post location. He's right. Blowfish signals to us with a repetitive pointing of his finger out the window. We've arrived.

The terrain around our post looks no different from any other sections of the miles of desert we have just passed. It's bushes and sandy mud as far as the eye can see. There is a cattle fence running from north to south, cutting across the Alpha line. Roger says the illegals follow the route of the fence as they make their way northward. He says we'll set up our lawn chairs in a way that we can see the fence. We walk toward the thicket behind us, where Tom has finally finished parking the van, to take out the gear.

Tom spent time a great amount of time maneuvering his van between a set of mesquite trees. He wanted to make sure it was concealed. The new van is all scratched up. Tom takes notice. He isn't too pleased about it, but he's also not too upset. It seems to add to his sense of self-worth—a sign of his sacrifice to the nation.

Tom is not finished ensuring the van doesn't blow our cover. He takes out a large camouflage netting from the trunk. We drape it over the side of the van—the side that's facing the border. Tom says it's the only side that matters. He remains concerned. The silver lining that surrounds the doors is showing. With the sun shining directly at it, it causes a reflection. He is frustrated and tinkers with the netting. Eventually he gives up. Anyway, the sun will be coming down soon enough.

Tom's concern shifts from our van to the pickup truck parked down the line at the other post. They haven't taken enough precautions with it. "They might as well be holding a neon sign that says 'Here We Are,'" Tom complains. He is concerned that the other post will blow our own cover. "This always happens," he says, clearing his runny nose with a swallow of mucus. "Someone who doesn't know what they're doing blows it for the entire line." Tom walks toward the other post, hands in pockets. His walk is slow and serious.

Roger and I grab the equipment: folding chairs, flashlights, radios, and night-vision scopes. For nourishment we have bottles of water, granola bars, and sandwiches. Roger has made some peanut butter and jelly sandwiches; Tom, his own special trail mix concoction of chocolate, cranberries, and nuts. The sun has melted it into a sticky mess. The food situation is not so straightforward. You can't bring anything that makes noise. That means nothing that really involves significant chewing. Plastic bags are to be brought with caution. They crinkle. Potato chips are not allowed.

Tom is upset. There's a full moon out. The emptiness of the desert makes the moon seem gigantic as it hangs at what appears to be a mere 50 feet above our heads. The moon is too bright for Tom's liking. That, combined with the blanket of stars, lights up the sky too much. "The illegals can spot us too easily," he declares.

Even though I explain that I have had some experience with it, Tom teaches me how to use the night-vision scope. He says his son, who is roughly my age, doesn't support what he's doing on the border. He says he has a rough relationship with him. His son is a "liberal." He works as the manager of a number of high-profile music bands, and Tom says that he could never bring his son down to the border with him—neither his son nor his wife. Tom says that whenever they go camping his wife complains. She's more of a "home-body," he tells me.

Tom tells me that the most important thing to remember with the night-vision scope is to never turn it on until its view-finder is flush against your eye. When the night vision is turned on, it emits a sharp neon light, which, if uncovered, extends far out into the distance. Tom says that the light will blow your cover, and "if there's a sniper out there, he can take you out with that light."

Tom tenderly explains that the weird blurry sensation you experience when you remove your eye from the scope lasts only a few seconds as the eye adjusts back to the reality of the dark night. But my weapons training is cut short.

Tom's cold has gotten the best of him. His condition has been deteriorating throughout the night. His coughs are now coming at five-second intervals and they make his whole body heave. I am concerned about his state. I think about how we are sitting motionless in the frigid weather. I imagine he must be suffering terribly. I tell him he shouldn't have gone out on patrol.

Tom nods in agreement. He fights off another cough. He says it's true; he shouldn't have come out on patrol, sick as he is. But instead of telling me, as I expect and as my question insinuated, that it's because he is suffering, he says it's because his coughing is "ruining the whole operation." The answer gives me pause. It is hard for me to comprehend the intense seriousness with which Tom takes sitting there on the border, the amount of suffering he is willing to go through for this. His intensity belies the fundamental difference in the ways we are experiencing the patrol. I am here to write a book; Tom is here to save America. Unlike me, he is experiencing this as a military operation. He feels he has a duty and obligation to keep quiet, and this experience, the experience of being in a situation where you should not cough even though you need to, holds a remarkable appeal.

But Tom can't take it anymore. With the cold weather pounding and his body heaving back and forth from violent coughs, he tells me in a whisper that he is going to walk to the van. He is hesitant to do it. But he will do it very carefully, very quietly. He will do it so that he can get a pillow from his trunk. He will use the pillow to muffle the sounds of his coughs.

Tom is now coughing into his pillow. Roger has woken up. He says that he is going to take Tom to the hospital tomorrow. He thinks they'll have to wait for hours because it'll undoubtedly be teeming with illegals. Tom wonders out loud if there's a VFW hospital in Tucson. As far as he knows, they don't treat illegals at those, "at least not yet," he irritably adds.[1]

Another hour of cold. Another hour of silence. Every few minutes, Tom lets out a barrage of coughs and quickly muffles them with the pillow. He's suffering. But with this suffering, I've come to realize, comes a sense of satisfaction: he is suffering for America.

The Border as a War Zone

I prepare to make what I hope is the final ascent up another rocky hill. A huge rock scrapes up against the bottom of my car. I was cautioned about attempting the drive in a sedan. The last time I was on a paved road was over forty-five minutes ago.

I descend the hill, miles upon miles of rough desert surround me. I'm a long way from the Anvil Ranch. There are no reporters down here. There aren't even many volunteers. It's a select few. It's some of the highest-status members in the group. They've come to a small swath of private land that sits right up against Mexico in order to build their own border fence. When completed, the fence will go for 0.9 miles. That's 0.9 miles of the 2,000-mile-long border.

There are a few small figures in the distance. My first thought is that it must be cattle. But cattle have no business in this rocky terrain. I notice something yellow. I squint. It's a forklift. Next to it there's a latrine. And then a set of cots. And then a couple of people. They look pathetically small against the backdrop of the seemingly endless Valley landscape that stretches in every direction around them.

Jack gives me a wave from afar. Along with Jack are Andrew and Mark. Mark is lying down on one of the cots, staring up at the sky, his arms folded behind his head. The sky has more going on than the desert in front of him. Andrew is standing next to Jack. As I drive up closer I notice a small grill set up next to one of the cots. There is something sad about seeing the three of them there, utterly alone.

Jack walks over to me as I park my car. We're about 50 feet from Mexico. The international border fence, the one made of the Vietnam era landing strips, came to an abrupt end about ten minutes ago when federal land ended and private land began. Now it's just a barbed wire fence. About half a mile past the fence, on the other side—the Mexican side—there's a set of railroad tracks.

Jack greets me. Mark is still lying on the cot. He's never been very fond of my presence and appears to purposefully pretend he doesn't notice me. Jack introduces me to Andrew, who is in his mid-thirties. He is originally from Boston but has spent the past fifteen years living in upstate New York. He has a thick Boston accent that comes out even though his bottom lip is crowded with chewing tobacco. He's short and walks with a limp and a cane. I've been told he was in Iraq during the first Gulf War, and I assume the limp is a war wound.

Jack is in charge of the fence project. He is a physically daunting figure. In many ways, he looks very different from the other Minutemen. He's physically fit and, at forty-three, relatively young. In fact, I notice that all three of them, Jack, Mark, and Andrew, are much younger than the Minutemen back at the camp.

Jack has bushy, curly hair and wears tight, cut-off jeans and shirts whose sleeves he's torn off. There's a machoness about him, and you can tell he works to give off that impression.

When he's not camping out here at the "fence site," as the Minutemen call it, Jack wakes up at 5 a.m. and makes a one-hour drive from his home. He gets up with the sun, when it's still cold outside. He says he likes to see the morning dew on the ground. And when he gets up Jack is very excited to get down to this place next to the border. He's too excited to even eat breakfast and instead packs himself a sandwich and a thermos of coffee. When he talks about working on the fence, unless he's probed, there's little in the way of mentioning of politics. He mentions the feel of lifting concrete slabs, of the dirt that gets in his face. These qualities of the job draw him to the undertaking.

Jack is originally from a rural part of western Virginia. He moved to Arizona in the late 1990s because his girlfriend's family is from here. He met Chris Simcox in Tombstone and says he was "kind of sucked into things." He is one of the original members of the group from back in 2002, back when it was called the Tombstone Militia, back when it had marginal press coverage, back when the membership consisted of about ten local residents.

Jack wants to show me the fence they're building. We take a walk around. He lights a cigarette. I do the same. Jack has a macho way of smoking, taking long drags and clamping the cigarette between his thumb and index finger so that when he smokes the cigarette itself is hidden, cupped inside his hand. Often he'll exhale through his nostrils. But as we begin our walk, I notice also that Jack wears thin metallic glasses that betray the rest of his appearance. I notice just how bushy and long his hair his. And I notice that he constantly uses the word "dude" and "man." He's a coalition of contradictory features. If I saw him in another context, I might pit him for a hippie.

The fence they're building is "Israeli style." They have blueprints of the fence that Israel has built along its border with the West Bank and Gaza, and Jack tells me they are following those specifications. He says he admires that fence and wants to reproduce it here in the desert. He meticulously lays out the design plan for me, which includes two parallel fences with a dirt road running in between them. He says that it's being designed in consideration of the Border Patrol; they will make the road wide enough so that the Border Patrol can drive through and even make a U-turn if they need to.

Jack knows I'm originally from Israel, and he wants to know if I've seen the fence over there. I nod. He looks at me as if I were a consultant, waiting to hear some insight. He mentions how successful the fence over there has been. "It's reduced terrorist attacks by something like 95 percent, isn't that right?" He asks me if I think they're doing a good job with theirs—if it "looks like the one over there." I look around. I see a couple of metal beams sticking out from the ground. I see a set of concrete slabs lying on the earth. I see some piles of wire mesh. I don't want to hurt Jack's feelings and so I pause, unsure of how to respond. Jack senses this. He interrupts my internal conversation. "I mean I know we're not there yet, but you've got to use your imagination."

Jack comes to a sudden halt. He doesn't want me to write up what he's about to tell me. He tells me it's off the record.[2] I brace myself. I anticipate a story of how the Minutemen killed a Mexican. I anticipate the "truth," which up to now I've only heard rumors about in the liberal media.

Jack was on patrol, back in the days of the Tombstone Militia, with two other people. One of them was a "good guy," but there was concern about the third. "We said to ourselves, what are we going to do with this guy?" Seriousness overtakes Jack's face. He's telling me a war story. He lights another cigarette. "Man, this guy was a psycho dude, he was totally out of control." There's tension on Jack's face. He takes an extended drag from his cigarette before starting up again. "You know we stopped this group, we had women there, there were a couple of babies, and we're there, the three of us. And I'm thinking to myself, what if this mother fucker takes out his gun and goes for them?" He pauses. Looks directly into my eye. "And you know what, man," he flicks his cigarette toward the "Israeli fence," "what I decided is that I would shoot that guy and walk away." Jack looks away. He's unsettled by the words that have just come out of his mouth.

I'm taken aback. I'm taken aback not only by the content of the story but also by the emotional sensitivity that's gushing out of Jack. I don't want to, but I know that I have to say something. I take a cue from Jack and light up my own cigarette. "No, come on man, you wouldn't shoot someone just like that," I say, reminding myself that we aren't talking about a Mexican but a fellow Minuteman. "If he started shooting up the Mexicans, hell yeah. I swear dude, I wouldn't think about it, if that guy was to start going at the Mexicans, with those women there, I would take that fucker out and walk away, clear conscience."

We continue to tour the nonexistent fence. Every now and then Jack makes a comment about what will be built at such and such location. I ask him if he's scared when he goes out on patrol, if he's ever worried that he will come across an armed drug runner. He says that the border is a dangerous place. People don't understand this, especially the "liberals." "Not all the people coming across are good people looking for a job. You know we got these druggies, these people trafficking prostitutes. It's not all poor José Sanchez trying to make ends meet, you know what I mean?" And as he tells me this, I wonder who he is trying to convince, me or him. What is clear to me is that it is very important for Jack to believe that there are "druggies" and "people trafficking prostitutes."

Jack often wonders about what he would do if there were a shootout. He says that "a potential encounter with drug runners carrying AK-47s" is something that's constantly on his mind. "It's a split-second decision, it's an instantaneous decision," he tells me. "You're in the moment and you gotta go with what you're feeling right there, but man, listen, I thank God I haven't had to be in that spot and I hope to God I won't ever have to."

Jack calls what's happening in America a "nuclear war." There's hyperbole in his voice to match the hyperbole of the image. I take him up on the imagery, "So what's the nuclear bomb and what's the mushroom cloud gonna look like?" He scratches his cheek with the back of his right hand. There's bushy hair growing out of his knuckles. For Jack the problem is different groups coming together beyond a breaking point. "What I've learned is that they're not a different race but a different ethnicity. . . . It's the intermixing of the ethnicities, man, it can't be sustained. We're putting together people with different ways of living, different loyalties, and it's a fucking struggle of the fittest man."

I tell Jack that one of the strengths of "our country"—I make sure to use the word "our"—is that it brings together people from different places. I tell him that our strength lies in our diversity. For Jack, too, diversity is important, "But we need to sustain the idea of America, of there being an American way. There needs to be an American way or we're nothing. It's the breakdown of society."

For Jack one of the big problems in America today is political correctness. "All this p.c. culture, these days you have to watch what you say, and in so doing you're losing your country." He is proud at the words coming out of his mouth. "The minute you feel like you can't express what you believe, it's over, man. No more America. The minute I feel like I gotta think twice about what I feel, I've lost my autonomy." He makes reference to George Orwell: "It's like in that book *1984*, that's what America has become. People are afraid to talk; the government is bringing everyone down. People are afraid of doing things. You can't be a citizen anymore."

Jack and I walk back to where Andrew and Mark are. Andrew asks me what I think of the fence. I tell him it seems like a big undertaking. Mark gets up from his cot and finally begins to make himself known. He tells me about the previous night. About how they caught three illegals. Mark is very excited while telling me this. I can tell he's lost some of his normal guarded way of talking with me. Just like the encouragement "good hunting," which is sometimes passed around before the patrols, "you're not supposed to use the word 'caught,' at least not back at the camp, at least not when the media are present. "We don't catch them," the leadership always says to me, "we just observe and report." But many rank-and-file volunteers, in different degrees, want to "catch" them. And when their guard is down, when their public selves are left behind, another vocabulary emerges: "catch," "hunt," "enemy," "make sure to get 'em with the light right between the eyes." The front-stage Minutemen rhetoric, the rhetoric of Chris Simcox, is the language of border management. But the backstage rhetoric is the language of warfare. And Jack, Andrew, and Mark are not there as politicians engaged in a project of managing the border; they are there as soldiers defending the nation.

They are using the night-vision binoculars—Generation-3, Mark adds. It's advanced technology; "you see things like it's the middle of the day."

Mark is in his late thirties. He lives outside of Philadelphia, where he works as an electrician. He is a former member of the Marine Corps, but don't tell him that; "one is never an ex-marine" he always says. Mark has a Marine Corps tattoo on his right shoulder. On the left one he's recently added a Minutemen tattoo. He looks and acts like he's still in the Marine Corps. His head is shaved, and when he goes out on patrol he dons more military equipment than anyone else. And he spends nearly all his money on it. He recently purchased a new bulletproof vest, which cost him over $1,000. Proudly, he tells me that it has a thick Kevlar plate. He says it could stop a shotgun bullet, even from close range.

Mark points to the top of the hill. He was perched up there last the night in order to get a good view. He interrupts his account to point out the train tracks on the other side of the border. He says that the train conductor is "working with us." I ask him what he means. He says that the conductor honks his horns if there are illegals on the train, ostensibly signaling to the Minutemen that there will be people trying to cross. Moreover, when there are drug runners on board he honks three times. Mark has never actually talked to the conductor, but he's come to this conclusion based on his imagination. He claims that in the past, a few hours after the conductor honked the horn, illegals have crossed. Yesterday the conductor honked.

Mark says that he did a lot of scoping of the area the past weeks, trying to pick out the best spot at which to wait for the illegals. As he sees it, there are two good options. One is to sit on the roof of his truck; the other is to sit at the top of the hill. Both provide him with a good angle to see down below. But the rooftop of the car doesn't offer cover. "You'd be too exposed," he tells me, as if offering advice. "So I'm hunkered down up there on the hill." He continues his account of the other night: "I've got a great vantage point on everything down below, and boom, there they were. A group of three of them. I hit 'em with the lights." Mark is giddy. "You should have seen the looks on their faces, stopped dead in their tracks."

Andrew asks if I want to see "where they came through." He says the footprints are still fresh. Andrew and I start walking. He's got his cane. Somehow the cane only makes him more intimidating. He rarely speaks, and when he does he is curt and matter-of-fact. His voice conveys only a cold, calm seriousness.

I ask Andrew how he got started with the Minutemen. He says, "9/11." He used to work in the World Trade Center. He knew about "a hundred guys who were killed." He calls 9/11 a "turning point." The day after 9/11 he sat down for a talk with his wife. "I told her, you know, if they need volunteers I'll do it. I was ready to enlist. I meant it. And I still mean it. I got this bum leg, but I would serve my country in a heartbeat." Andrew says that after 9/11 he felt like he "needed to do something."

Andrew and I are right up against the barbed wire fence. "There they are," Andrew says as he points with his cane to a set of footprints in the mud directly below a bent portion of the barbed wire fence. I walk down to take a closer inspection. As I look out into Mexico, he warns me, "I wouldn't cross that line, because they'll shoot you."

I'm standing with Andrew. We're facing the empty stretch of desert that is Mexico. And suddenly a helicopter comes at us. It is coming from our left, to the west, over the top of a mountain. It shuttles toward us, straddling the barbed wire fence that separates one stretch of desert from another.

KARL HOFFMAN

Mark is lying on his cot. Jack is standing next to his truck. They are 200 feet away from Andrew and me. Andrew looks at the helicopter. He tells me it looks like the Border Patrol. He waves. I wave as well. Just as the helicopter flies overhead, Andrew tells me that he didn't notice any Border Patrol logo on it. He finds it curious. Andrew and I turn to see the helicopter continue its flight path, straddling the U.S.-Mexico border.

Mark rushes toward us. "Hey, did that helicopter have any writing on it?" There's desperation in his voice. Andrew says it did not, seemingly happy that his own observations have been confirmed. "Yeah, that's what I thought," Mark continues in haste. "It was fucking unmarked. It was a Mexican fucking military helicopter."

Jack races to his truck. He takes out two pistols from inside, and with his back kneeling on the driver's side door he cocks them both. Mark makes a run to his own truck, pulls out his bulletproof vest, and proceeds to strap it on. Andrew hobbles in haste. He falls on the way. I help him up. He gives me an admiring glance. We make a run for Jack's truck, where Mark is now also hunkered down. The exhilaration is contagious. The fear, the excitement, is intense. Everyone has at least one gun in their hands. Jack yells out, "They're coming at us tonight, they're fucking coming at us." Mark puts a fresh clip into his gun. "There's gonna be a god damn shoot-out tonight." All of us are crouching beside Jack's truck.

I am confused. For a second I think to myself that they don't *really* think that was a Mexican military helicopter and that the Mexican military is coming for them but are just toying with me, and that at some point they will stop and say, "Just kidding." But I recall a previous conversation I had with Mark. Knowing that I was a student in New York, Mark once asked me if I had "an escape plan." Thinking he was referring to life after graduate school, I told him I was looking forward to getting a teaching job. He laughed. "I mean, how the fuck are you gonna get out of there when shit hits the fan? How are you gonna get off that island? You got a contingency plan for if the highways are all shut down?" And then it dawns on me, very strongly, that this is no ploy. They really do think that was a Mexican helicopter. I think this is absurd. I think they are crazy. I want to laugh. But then I am also scared. Their reactions are seductive. My own point of view is overtaken by theirs. I wonder if I should ask Jack for one of his guns. I wonder if I should make a run for the latrine and hide inside. I wonder if I should be afraid of the Mexicans or the Minutemen.

Mark says he isn't "hard core enough for this." He says, "If they start coming at us with fucking tanks, I'm outta here guys. I am not dying for this. I've got a wife back home. I mean, I'll be down here and patrol, but I'm not taking on the fucking Mexican army, that's where I draw the line."

Between the fear and exhilaration, there's an intimacy among the four of us, hunkered down in the space beside Jack's truck. There's a shared sense of honor, of dedication, of protection, and fear. We're in this together.

But nothing happens. The enemy doesn't attack.

A minute passes. Then another. I wonder at what point the moment will pass. I wonder at what point they'll put away their guns and feel safe enough to walk around in this empty space.

Mark is suddenly very talkative. His curtness is now completely gone. He is ranting. He's letting it all spill out. It's a catharsis. "Mexican culture is backwards. If I were poor I wouldn't have so many fucking babies, but that's what they do. It's fucking despicable. But over there it's a macho thing. You know, you show how many kids you can have, that's what it means to be a man, to be macho."

I ask him why the helicopter flew over us. He says it was probably a scout to see where the Minutemen were and how many of them there were. He says it happens often. The Mexican military is always scouting them. He thinks they might be coming after the Minutemen. But there's also another possibility, "Maybe they also want to know where we are so they know where to bring the illegals so they can cross."

The stories of Mexican military plotting to attack the Minutemen are commonplace among the Minutemen. A few months back, when the Minutemen spotted a cavalry of Mexican military personnel driving along the border, one of the volunteers sent out an emergency message to all other Minutemen: "Confirmed only moments ago, Mexican Military have set up only yards from the border across from a Minutemen post. . . . Unknown number of soldiers/drug smugglers at this point, they are hidden and being watched carefully as I write this."

A volunteer on his way to participate in the patrols responded, "Keep your heads down tonight and watch behind you as closely as your front.

I was worried about snakes. Now I'm worried about my wife finding out about this. She would support me anyway. My father told me that one day I may have to stand up for what I believe in. When I get there on Friday I'll get to find out if that day has arrived. When you're my size, you don't scare anyone. But, this long-haired, four-eyed old man will be standing up for what he believes in. So save me a space on line OK? . . . Stay safe and you are all in my prayers tonight."

We hear a vehicle barreling toward us. It's Chris Simcox, in his expensive SUV.

One by one the men get up from the bunker. One by one they put their guns in their holsters.

The fear seems to have suddenly vanished. But why? I'm confused. Chris parks his car. As he hops out, so too do two Alaskan huskies. They rampage about. The men are happy to see Chris. Mark walks up to him and shakes his hand. "El Presidente!" he jokes.

Chris takes out a brand-new tent from the back of his car and hands it to Mark. "Guess what else I've got for you guys?" The men look on eagerly as Chris displays two thermal scopes. I can tell Chris is a bit unsettled by my being down here. He's always told me I've got an open account to do as I like, but I sense he is not pleased by my presence. He didn't expect me down here.

I'm waiting for the men to recount the story of the helicopter. I'm waiting for them to tell Chris about the moment of reckoning that almost took place. But they don't. Not only have they put away their guns, but they have also put away their panic. They walk and talk as if nothing happened. I almost want to tell Chris about it myself. And then Mark does it. "You just missed it man, we just had an unmarked helicopter fly over head, don't know if it was Mexican military or drug scouts." He speaks with eagerness, but it's done in a mostly restrained tone. There is only a small trace of the previous emotion. When Chris responds, I start to understand the change in the men's behavior, "Oh, okay," he says, gives a snide patronizing smile, and, as if he feels compelled to say something, continues in an offhand way, "well, we knew this was a dangerous place."

If they were looking for recognition of the threat they witnessed, they weren't going to get it from Chris. And they seemed to know this. They seemed to understand that he wouldn't have seen things the same way, or approved of how they reacted. They needed to downplay what they had done. As I see these men change in front of Chris, I realize that when Chris came down, so too did something else: the organization. It wasn't the presence of the ethnographer who altered how these men behaved, but the presence of the president of the group.

The Border as a Phobia

Better known through his handle "Legolas," his favorite character in J.R.R. Tolkien's book *The Lord of the Rings*, Bruce is one of a select group of Minutemen who work as "scouts" or "trackers."

Like most other scouts, Legolas is younger than the volunteers who stand post on the line. A former member of the Marine Corps. and veteran of the first Gulf War, he is short and has a thick mustache and bushy hair. An avid player of fantasy games like *Dungeons and Dragons*, Legolas is very much a child at heart. Of everyone at the camp, he takes the most care and pleasure in referring to people only by their handles.

As Legolas explains it, the scouts do "recon work." "Our job is to find the places where the illegals are coming from, figure out where they are moving, and which areas give us good cover and the best chance of spotting them." The scouts do not have the same kinds of restrictions placed on them as those who stand post: they neither have to follow the same routine schedule nor have to remain motionless. Indeed, the foundation of their job is mobility.

The scouts' work takes place during the daylight hours. In part it is because their task demands good lighting; in part it's because scouting provides these men, who will not stand post during the morning shift, but who are likely to go on the graveyard shift, with something to do during the day.

"It's about being able to read the signs," Legolas tells me. Reading the signs, or "cutting signs," as it is known in more technical terminology, refers to interpreting various disturbances in the desert terrain. Legolas learned to read signs back in the army, and he first put his skills to use in the deserts of Iraq. Now he's putting them to use in the deserts of southern Arizona.

As I'm trekking through the desert with Legolas, he explains, with his words and body, the work involved. "You see those there," he says as he points to a set of footprints, "those are fresh ones. You can tell because you can still see the indentations real clear." I ask for more detail, and Legolas is eager to oblige. He sees himself as an expert in the matter and speaks with the authority of one. "Basically when the illegals come by, their footprints will stay for a couple of days before they get covered up. Of course that all depends on the weather. During the monsoons you've got no hope of tracking them because they'll get washed right up." He gets down on one knee and makes a closer inspection of the footprints. He looks up at me from the ground. "But when it's dry they can stay for a long time. And depending on how clear the indent is, you can get a pretty good sense of how long ago they came through."

Legolas gets up and smacks the dirt off his hands. He directs me to take a close look at the footprints. "You see how they are not all the same?" Noticing a variation in the size of the shoe prints, I nod. "Well," he says matter-of-factly, "that's how you can tell how many of them there were. You can see that over here." He pauses and scans over the ground. "We've got, I'd say a group of probably four of them."

But there is more. "If they're real clear, you can also get a sense of who these people are." I give him an inquisitive look. "Well, if you've got a small print you know it's either a child or a woman. And a deep print is a good sign that the person's probably carrying a load." In the language of patrol, as I'd learned, "carrying a load" meant carrying drugs.

Excited by my attentiveness and his ability to display knowledge, Legolas tells me that "you can even figure out in which direction they're heading." He stomps his ankle-high army boots into the earth, does a sharp 90-degree turn with his heel, and looks at me. "You see that? You see how the heel is curved like that?" I nod and he continues, "Well, that means that I've made a turn and headed that way," pointing into the eastern desert.

Legolas may be tracking, but he is it not going to find anyone. And even on those rare occasions when he does, he isn't going to do anything except maybe call the Border Patrol. The meaning of the "track" is to be found in the present, in the act of tracking, not in any future encounter. It is from trekking through this desert, getting on the ground, and using his skills that Legolas gets meaning out of cutting signs. The meaning is in the practice. It is in making patrolling the border part of his life, part of what he does, and what he is. And it is a satisfaction connected to a sense that he is a soldier and this is a war.

When cutting signs, Legolas is constructing the desert as a war zone and producing a relationship between himself, the soldier, and José, the enemy. It is a practice that revolves around getting to know the enemy, getting to know how many of them there are and where they are headed. It is about gathering information for an impending war, a war that Legolas will not be engaged in. And of the information collected about the enemy, the most important is the information about the enemy's moral character. Nowhere else is the moral character of the enemy displayed better than in the layup sites.

Deep in the desert, hidden inside caves, on the sides of washes, or between a tightly packed group mesquite trees, are layup sites, so called by the Minutemen, Border Patrol agents, and locals alike. They are the campsites of illegal immigrants as they make their way across the desert. In every direction it's a sea of personal effects. But not just any. They are the belongings of a people on the run, a people moving through the desert. Water bottles. Blankets. Canned tuna. Jackets. Toothbrushes. Soap. Toilet paper. And backpacks. Piles and piles of backpacks. Not one. Not two. But tens, perhaps hundreds. These are the flophouses of the global economy. And for the Minutemen, they are places invested with enormous meaning. It is a meaning that helps establish why their patrols matter, a meaning based on their interpretations of what these sites are, and what they tell us about the people coming across the border.

Legolas has seen this layup site before. "It's a popular one," he tells me. "We discovered it about six months ago while scouting." The two of us make our way around the camp, ducking to avoid the mesquite trees, keeping our eyes on the ground to make sure we don't stumble on a piece of debris.

Suddenly Legolas puts his hand out, motioning for me to stop, and then to lie low. He puts his index finger on his lips, signaling for me to be quiet. He asks me if "I hear that." I tell him I hear nothing. He says that the sound was a "turkey call." As if the meaning was self-explanatory, he doesn't say anymore. I had heard that people hunt for wild game in the Valley, but, as I tell Legolas, "I didn't know there were any wild turkeys around here." He chuckles. "No, no. The coyotes have scouts they send out ahead of the group, to scope things out. And when they see us they send signals to the group not to move." Apparently seeing the confusion on my face, he continues, "Oh, you bet, it happens all the time. There's probably a guy right out there," he says, pointing to the desert ahead, "with a pair of binoculars looking right at us."

Legolas directs me to the branches of one of the trees. There's a bra hanging from it. "You see that there? Pardon my language, but that's what's called a rape tree."

We move closer to the tree. "What the coyotes do is they take the women they're with," Legolas says, almost like a tour guide, "and they rape them." Even though I'd heard the story of "rape trees" many times before, I raise my eyebrows to give him the satisfaction of the shock he was looking to provoke. "That's right. It's part of their fee. They'll take them and rape 'em. I've been out on patrol and I've heard it myself. Heard the screams of some poor woman being taken advantage." He pauses in contemplation. "It's sickening, just sickening."

The rape tree exists as a central trope in the Minutemen imaginary of the border, and of the people who are crossing. As another member recounts in an e-mail sent out to volunteers with a photo of a tree with a woman's bra hanging from one of the branches, "On Tuesday, April 17th, a routine event took place on the border. The victim, statistics show, was young, female, and of Latin American descent. . . . 'Rape Trees' are a visible reminder of the dangers of our unsecured borders. . . . The 'coyote' committed a crime when he took advantage of a defenseless woman in his care. He raped the young woman and went away bragging about his machismo to his peers. He left his mark, the woman's bra, cut between the 'cups,' on the tree for all to see how big a man he is. . . . This is part of his culture and an accepted part of his business." The rape tree works to construct the Minutemen's own acts as patriotic deeds as it simultaneously constructs the illegal immigrants' acts as immoral.

But as the case of the rape tree shows, not everyone who crosses the border is immoral. In this scenario, the immorality of the coyote is pitted against not just the morality of the Minuteman, but also the innocence of the female crosser. The coyote's immorality is rooted in a notion of a depraved masculinity. In such a manner, the border is constructed as a stage of competing masculinities: the Minutemen's virtuous masculinity, based on protecting the troubled female, is pitted against the coyote's vile machismo. For the Minutemen, the rape trees are a powerful symbol of the Mexican male's immorality and simultaneously imbue their own actions with valor; by patrolling the border, the volunteers are defending not just America but women, and not just American women but all women, even the ones who are "illegal."

As Legolas and I continue to tour the site, I bend down to inspect a backpack. Legolas cautions me, "I wouldn't touch it with your bare hands. It's got all kinds of disease on it." I recoil a bit. Legolas walks over, his boots crushing over backpack after backpack. Standing next to me, he takes off his own backpack. His is army issued. It is a sophisticated item: chest straps, waist straps, Velcro latches, pockets in every direction, padding in every corner, a special internal compartment for water, and everything is coated in camouflage.

He sits the backpack on the ground, opens it up and removes what I think is a box of tissues. But I am mistaken. It's a box of plastic gloves, the kind surgeons wear. He stretches one of the gloves onto his right hand. "This is the only way I touch this stuff," he tells me.

Of the many ways the Minutemen talk about José, disease is a common trope and anchors the xenophobia in their politics. In metaphorical

ANDREA DYLEWSKI

terms they speak of the "illegals" as a "cancer"; they talk about how they "bring over a backwards culture," "a diseased way of life." But just as the fear the Minutemen feel is not just an existential one but a real physical one, so too are the diseases they say the illegals bring across the border. "You know what kinds of diseases they're bringing over?" Legolas rhetorically asks me. "I mean we've got cases of things like leprosy and TB, stuff that's been wiped out for generations and now it's coming back in."

Back home the volunteers will talk of not eating at restaurants where they suspect illegal immigrants are working; here at the layup sites they wear gloves; on patrol they are cautioned never to touch an illegal. The Minutemen's brand of xenophobia really is a phobia.

Legolas bends down and inspects a pill bottle. With gloves in hand, he opens up the bottle and carefully shakes out a couple of white pills. "You know what these are?" he looks up at me from his knees. He tells me they are "birthing pills." I assume that he means birth control pills, and that where he comes from they just go by another name. But I am wrong. "Yeah, you see, what the women who cross do is, a lot of them cross when they are pregnant, and basically they take these pills which induce labor. They know that if they give birth to someone in the States they get to stay here." He pauses. "And they call themselves mothers."

I am confused. Not simply about whether these "birthing pills" are real or not; I doubt that they are. I'm confused about how Legolas went from talking about the women who cross as victims just a few minutes ago to suddenly talking about them as immoral. But while these two interpretations of the women coming across the border are contradictory, they cohere to a central logic: the Minutemen matter. Whether it's defending the illegal immigrant woman who is being raped or stopping the illegal immigrant woman who is taking birthing pills, the meaning is the same: we need to be here, and we are doing good. But these depictions of José also do more than justify the Minutemen's presence; they also reflect a vision of what the danger is and what the Minutemen's role is in warding it off. In the minds of the Minutemen, their presence on the border serves as a moral bulwark against the pollution and contamination of the body politics—the nation is a family, and the Minutemen are the patriarchs.

In her analysis of dietary regulations, Mary Douglas (1966) suggests that things are never inherently "dirty" but rather get constituted as such.[3] Further, what is constituted as a polluting agent in one society or context may not be in another. But behind these differences in the object is a common structure. Things constituted as dirty are things that have no clear place in the social order. They are things that do not have a clear place in the categories with which we organize the world: that which is dirty is that which is unclassifiable.

But José Sanchez is not unclassifiable. Although a contradictory figure—at once a good worker and a rapist—this is not the force behind his conception as a polluting agent. The character of José the polluting agent is very clear, very classifiable: it is the rapist, the criminal. José is the opposite of the unclassifiable; he is the classifiable outsider who helps constitute the insider. And this is what vexes the Minutemen. Deep down they know José is not evil, but he must be made immoral, unclean, if their pursuit is to have any meaning.[4]

Legolas opens up the side pocket of his backpack. He takes out a ziplock bag. Curious to see what the bag is for, I watch as he carefully puts the pills inside and then puts the bag in his backpack. Noticing my stare, he explains that he often takes what he finds at a layup site and brings it back home. "They're kind of like little mementos."

From the Nativist's Point of View

What are we to make of these stories? How are we to interpret them, and how do they help us understand who the Minutemen are and what they are doing on the border?

The ambition of ethnographic knowledge is, as Clifford Geertz has classically put it, to provide the reader with access to how people see the world.[5] What ethnographers seek to gain by traveling to foreign worlds and spending significant time there—what they ultimately should provide their readers—is what Geertz calls a "thick description," an account of how people in those foreign worlds interpret and give meaning to those worlds. The goal is to see things from "the native's point of view." Without these thick descriptions, we might misunderstand the meaning behind what people in these worlds are doing. As Geertz put it, sometimes an act like a wink may mean one thing (flirting with someone), and sometimes it may mean another (sharing a secret with someone). To get it right, to interpret these acts correctly, whether they be winks or patrols, we need to understand the meaning they hold for those who are doing them.

Each of the previous stories, in one way or another, has to do with how the Minutemen see the border and, by extension, how they see themselves: they see both through the eyes of a soldier.

What the Minutemen are fundamentally after is an experience. It is a particular experience, one organized around soldiering. Belonging to the Minutemen and patrolling the border holds appeal not because it holds the possibility of enforcing immigration policy—that is not the meaning behind the act—but rather, because it holds the appeal of reliving the experience of soldiering.

On the one hand, these experiences are connected to a set of beliefs the Minutemen hold about José, but those beliefs are not enough to explain them. Whether it is Tom's cough, or Mark putting on his bulletproof vest, or Legolas cutting signs, the meaning of these acts can be understood only in the context of these men's past lives as soldiers. The meaning of soldiering is connected not to actually engaging in battle but to participating in a world where one goes on a "mission" that requires not coughing; where one feels like one is in a position to make a life-or-death decision; where one is able to use skills that can no longer be used in one's everyday life.

Jack talks about the existence of an "American way." Although he says that he is on the border because Mexicans don't represent the American way, he is actually on the border because he recognizes that *he* no longer represents the American way—or, more correctly, that his way of being in America is gone. And what he comes down to the border to reclaim is that way of being in America, a way where he feels at home, where he feels like he matters, where he is a soldier.

To a great extent the Minutemen are trying to extend their former identities. There is no clearer indication of this than Mark's tattooed shoulders. While Mark often claims that "one is never an ex-marine," what the two tattoos reveal is in fact the opposite. The new, Minuteman tattoo is there precisely because he is no longer a marine.

At the root of reclaiming this identity is the reclaiming of a lost sense of masculinity. Underneath a self-professed bravado, there is fear. They are terrified. In their imagination they are subject to violence but not agents of violence; worried about a violence that is always on the verge of being inflicted on them. And in their imagination they are the weaker party, fighting off terrorists, drug dealers, and rapists. This is not about "poor José Sanchez looking for work"; he's not what will provide them with the sense of masculinity they have lost.

In large part these men's trips to the border should be understood as pilgrimages: journeys and experiences in places set apart from their everyday lives where they get to experience a different sense of self.[6] They are escapes into other worlds, worlds removed from their everyday lives. They are escapes from worlds where they feel emasculated, worlds where they feel like they have no agency. What better world to escape to than one where they can be soldiers.[7]

Part of the challenge is to carry that sense of self back home with them—Tom takes a video, Legolas a memento. All of them take back an experience.

In some ways, José is crucial to this, while in other ways he is incidental. If José didn't exist, the Minutemen would invent him. And this is just what they do.

The meanings of objects that Minutemen encounter on their patrols do not come from objects themselves. To signify, these signs need to be, as Legolas puts it, "read." And as they involve an active process of reading, they also involve manipulation: the sign will be read from a particular viewpoint, translated in a way that supports the ends of the reader. The Minutemen take the desert's ambiguous signs and translate them into signals of danger or victimhood. They translate them in a way that sustains their practices, that sustains their patrols of the border as acts of patriotism.

It is Easter 2007. For the past five days there have been almost zero sightings, let alone apprehensions. A story circulates around the camp: it's Easter, and in Mexico they take Easter very seriously. Everyone is home with their families, and so it makes sense that no one is crossing. As Blowfish tells the men, "Let's wait it out, they'll be crossing in a few more days."

As the Minutemen interpret the situation, if there are apprehensions, they are effective. It means José has been caught and prevented from entering America. But if there are no apprehensions, they are also effective: it means they are stopping people from crossing. It means the Minutemen's presence has shut down this section of border. No matter what the "data," the practice of patrolling is rendered effective and meaning-ful. This is what we must understand if we are to understand what the Minutemen are doing on the border: they want to belong to a world where they can be the soldiers they once were. José offers them that chance. And that is the great irony of the Minutemen's patrols, of their efforts to stop José: the Minutemen need him; he is the basis of their experience. So long as José is out there, Tom must muffle his cough.

In his classic study of belief, *When Prophecy Fails*, Leon Festinger and his colleagues examine what happens when reality does not conform to people's expectations.[8] Focusing on a doomsday cult that organized around the belief that the world was coming to an end at a specific point in time, Festinger looks at what happens when our beliefs are disproven. Members of this cult believed that aliens were going to come to Earth on a particular day, and that they would be rescued from the impending doom. However, when the time comes, the aliens do not arrive and the world does not end. And yet Festinger finds something curious. The be-lievers did not take these as signs that their beliefs were wrong. Rather, they created accounts that rescued their beliefs. The calculations were done wrong; the preparations were incorrect. The problem, the leaders of the cult said, was not in the beliefs.

Festinger claims that when we hold strong beliefs and are confronted with information that appears to disprove our beliefs, we experience cog-nitive dissonance, a psychological tension between our beliefs and reality, that throws our identity out of balance. In an effort to repair this tension, we engage in reinterpretations of the information in such a way that what appears to disprove our beliefs actually ends up reconfirming them.

In Festinger's account, beliefs matter a great deal to people's sense of self. Lose the beliefs and you lose the core of your identity. What is at stake in disproving information is the status of the beliefs.

While it is certainly true that beliefs matter, they do not matter simply as ends in and of themselves. Beliefs are meaningless without the worlds to which they are connected. What is being rescued when disproven information is reinterpreted is not simply the status of the belief but the social world those beliefs sustain. When the Minutemen are faced with evidence that suggests that José may not be who they think he is, they reinterpret it, and they do so to rescue not simply an argument but an experience.

Sitting around the camp while sharing breakfast, Don reflects, "I haven't seen any terrorists come across. The only people I have seen are hardworking people." But another volunteer quickly interjects, "Well, it only takes one."

Think of George, a volunteer from Texas sharing a late-night coffee with a few other Minutemen. George says he "respects the illegals"; he calls them "honorable." Earlier in the day George saw an old man, an illegal immigrant, on the side of the road. "He had been beaten." We all lurched up at these words. Someone asked for more details. "Did you see who did it?" "No, I mean he was beaten by the *desert*, by the difficulty of it. I felt for him, you don't want to see a grown man like that. But what can I tell you, you feel bad, but he shouldn't be doing it in the first place."

At both these moments, the image of José the terrorist, José the enemy, is challenged by the image of José the hard worker, José the old man, and consequentially the meaning of what the Minutemen are doing on the border is also challenged. Could it be that they are not brave soldiers fighting a potent adversary but old men squabbling with other old men?

"It only takes one." "He shouldn't be doing it in the first place." What is being repaired by these statements? Is it a set of beliefs? Certainly. But it is also the patrols themselves and their meaning that the Minutemen struggle to rescue. If the encounter is the proclaimed goal of the mission, it is also the most dangerous moment. The Minutemen pose this danger as a physical one, but it is also an existential one. The danger for the Minutemen is that in encountering José, they also encounter themselves: weak, marginalized, and separated from the country they want to call their own.

KARL HOFFMAN

CHAPTER 5

Encounters

||||||||||||||||||

UNLIKE HEATHER, NURSE NANCY, and Brother John, I recognized the man standing at the head of the hill right away. While they were squinting, debating which of the four possible people you see around here he might be—Border Patrol agent, rancher, Minuteman, or illegal immigrant—I knew for sure. The suspenders gave him away. Fred always wore suspenders.

It was only a few days after I started my research that I heard about Heather, Nurse Nancy, and Brother John. They were members of the Samaritans, one of three affiliated but disputing groups,[1] each based out of churches in Tucson, that patrol the same stretch of the Valley as the Minutemen, but for radically different reasons. As Heather explained the difference to me, "We do it in order to provide humanitarian assistance to the migrants crossing the desert."

I debated for a long time whether I should spend time with the Samaritans. The Samaritans are undoubtedly an important part of the ecology of the border. Although Arizona often appears as a bastion of right-wing conservatism, where the passage of restrictive immigration laws suggests a place populated by people who welcome the Minutemen, here is a group that openly criticizes the Minutemen and that moves about in the exact same physical space. Indeed, the phenomenon of civilians patrolling borders, as the Samaritans' existence revealed to me, could not be understood just through a focus on the Minutemen. This was not simply a right-wing activity. Other people, with other agendas, were on the border. Who were they? What were *they* doing there? And how did they and the Minutemen deal with each other?

While the importance and benefits of spending time with the Samaritans were apparent, the repercussions were uncertain. I was sure there would be some, but what form they would take and how extensive they would be I didn't know. One thing was certain, I didn't want to damage my relationship with the Minutemen.

With these conflicts in mind, I decided, about six months into my fieldwork, to approach the Minutemen leadership and ask for their permission to go out and patrol the border a "couple of times" with members of the Samaritans. To my surprise they agreed, and they did so with encouragement. The encouragement took various forms: First, it was organized around a moral principle that the demands of "objective reporting" and my doing a "good job" for my dissertation required my "getting both sides of the story." Second, it involved a curiosity that was not simply innocent but contained a desire to enroll me in the search for self-serving strategic information, to "let us know what they are about" but also "make sure to tell us when you see them break the law." Finally, it showed a self-righteousness that accompanies people who believe ardently in the rationality of their own beliefs and behavior and the irrationality of those who oppose them, to "go for it, see how crazy they are."

Although I said so to the Minutemen leadership, I never intended to patrol the border with the Samaritans only a couple of times, and I didn't. Over the course of the next two years I spent over 250 hours on patrol with them and attended close to 100 organizational meetings. I also kept my time with them a complete a secret from almost all the rank-and-file Minutemen. Moreover, following a similar logic as that above, for the most part I also hid from the Samaritans the fact that I spent time with the Minutemen.

And here I was with Heather, Nurse Nancy, and Brother John, faced with the moment I had been dreading. It was April 2007, and we were about to cross paths with Fred, a well-respected member of the Minutemen, known back at the camp as much for his suspenders as for his anger about what he called the "open-border lobby"—a murky group of people, some politicians, some businessmen, some activists, all of them "liberals"—who he claimed sought to get rid of any kind of border be-tween the United States and Mexico. Or, as Fred would say, "to turn Mexico and America into one big country."

"It's a Minutemen-looking guy." Heather slowed her notoriously fast pace. Fred's camouflaged jacket, as well as the all-terrain vehicle that was hidden in the brush, were now clearly in view. Nurse Nancy's demeanor quickly changed. She had told me before about how she was afraid of the Minutemen, and I could tell she was anxious. Heather put one of her arms out, motioning to the rest of us to slow down. "Just smile and keep walking. It's not worth our time to start arguing with him."

My heart beating nervously, I put my head down while the they exchanged a few sarcastic pleasantries. Although no one directly an-nounced who they were, everyone seemed to know. The options were in-deed limited. And just as Fred, with his camouflage jacket and ATV, not to mention exposed sidearm, was "a Minuteman-looking guy," Heather, Nurse Nancy, and especially Brother John, wearing a Franciscan monk's robe, were decidedly *not* Minuteman-looking guys.

"So what is it you all do?" Fred's resentful tone indicated he clearly knew just who we were. But none of the Samaritans responded. They kept walking, and I was all too eager to do the same. But Fred couldn't let the moment pass. "You know," he fired back, "we *also* give them food and water. What *we* do," he continued, pausing for rhetorical ef-fect, "is we give the illegals food and water and then we call the Border Patrol".

Heather couldn't hold back. Succinctly and self-righteously, she turned to look back at Fred and replied, "Well, what *we* do is give them food and water and *ask* them if they want us to call the Border Patrol."

For the next hour, as I hiked the Arizona desert with Heather, Nurse Nancy, and Brother John, I thought about the exchange. In conversa-tions I had had with them, members of each group had usually accused members of the other of egregious criminal activities—the Minutemen accused the Samaritans of actively smuggling illegal immigrants into Arizona, while the Samaritans accused the Minutemen of forcibly de-taining, if not outright shooting, those whom they came across during their patrols. But my experiences on patrol had undermined the stories of detentions and smugglings I had been told. In the hundreds of hours I had spent patrolling the border with both groups, encounters with illegal immigrants were a rare occurrence. Yes, sometimes I witnessed the Samaritans putting an illegal immigrant in their car and providing assistance that went beyond giving food and water, and sometimes I saw the Minutemen do more than sit in their lawn chairs and call the Border Patrol. But these incidents were extremely rare—outliers from the norm, a norm that was much less radical than the one I supposed; one much less radical than the names "Samaritans" and "Minutemen" and the distinction of "humanitarian" and "vigilante" suppose.

But in Heather's and Fred's minds, there is a great difference between the two of them. They each see themselves as moral and the other as immoral. In large part they extrapolate these differences by focusing on the course of action they claim the other takes when they encounter illegal immigrants. On the one hand, they imagine the differences between what they do on patrol to be greater than they really are—that one smuggles illegal immigrants while the other shoots them. On the other hand, they also recognize what the real actions of each are on patrol—a difference in how they go about calling on the Border Patrol—and see this, as Heather suggests in her indignant tone, to be a mark of great difference.

As I have tried to argue throughout this book, the moment that Heather and Fred focus on when understanding each other and differentiating themselves is the wrong moment to focus on. It is exactly the kind of moment scholars and media, as well as the public, tend to investigate to understand these people: the Minutemen are those who stop illegal immigrants, and the Samaritans are those who help illegal immigrants. A focus on the moment of encounter is also exactly what the designations "humanitarian" and "vigilante" are built on. But these labels and these moments tell us very little about these people. The labels humanitarian and vigilante, and the encounters with José, reveal little about Heather and Fred.

The Samaritans are a challenge to the Minutemen. They use similar values and ideas (civic engagement, invasion) and do the same thing (patrol the border), but for different ends and against different enemies. And so too are the Samaritans a challenge for me, and for my argument.

Up to now, the argument that we need to look beyond the ideological foundations of political behavior to understand those behaviors, that we need to understand the practice of patrolling the border by connecting it to biographies, that we need to understand immigration politics as having to do not just with beliefs about immigration but with ways of being in the world, has been built around the Minutemen. I have made these claims by focusing not on the moment in which the Minutemen encounter José, but by focusing on how they prepare for these encounters, and by focusing on how these patrols fit into the volunteers' larger lives. What, if anything, can be revealed about the Samaritans by applying the same technique to them? What happens to our understanding of the Samaritans? To our understanding of the Minutemen?

History of an Encounter

That day in April 2007 when Heather's and Fred's paths crossed in the middle of the Arizona desert was the first time the two had ever met. But the truth is, Heather and Fred have been crossing each other's paths for many years; the truth is, they have been encountering each other throughout their whole lives.

Heather is sixty-six. Fred is sixty-eight. They came of age at the same time. Their stories of childhood are marked by similar events: their first television set growing up; watching the *Ed Sullivan Show* with their parents on that television set. And so too their stories of adulthood: the Vietnam war; the assassination of John F. Kennedy; the moon landing.

But they experienced these events in very different ways.

Heather looks much older than she is. Her face and hands are so wrinkled that it's hard to imagine that there was a time when they were not like that. She is thin and short. Her silvery grey hair runs wild.

Heather was born in Arizona. Her parents were both schoolteachers and active members of the Southside Presbyterian Church. "School and church," she says about her childhood, "those were the two big themes. . . . My parents were religious, but at the end of the day they saw them both as places to be educated. Whether I was reading the Bible or *Moby-Dick*, I grew up seeing them both as sources of knowledge."

At eighteen Heather left Arizona to attend a small women's college in the Northeast were she majored in literature. She describes the school she attended as "pretty left-wing," and it was there, she says, that she began to be politically engaged. Vietnam had started just a few years before. The women's movement was getting under way. And as Heather puts it, "I was at an all-women college where the women spoke their minds . . . there was a strong sense of sisterhood. . . . From the first day I stepped on campus there were protests going on. And each year it seemed like there was just more and more of it."

At college Heather remained active in church life, often leading trips to a nearby Presbyterian church. And when students at the college organized a trip to Washington, D.C., to protest the war, she took the lead in organizing the various church groups.

Reflecting back on her involvement in the anti–Vietnam War movement, Heather says the My Lai massacre of 1968, when U.S. soldiers murdered close to five hundred unarmed civilians, soldiers, was a turning point. "I just remember seeing these images of dead bodies, babies, young women, just spread out on the ground. Piles and piles . . . I mean what the hell were we doing there? Who were fighting? Poor villagers?"

After college she returned to her native Arizona, where she received a master's degree in education and continued her involvement in antiwar protests as well as the Southside Presbyterian Church, which she had attended growing up. She eventually married and found a job as a part-time instructor at a local community college.

In the early 1980s civil war was engulfing Central America, and thousands of people from Guatemala and El Salvador fled to the United States in search of asylum. But they were not granted asylum. In response, Reverend John Fife, then minister of the Southside Presbyterian Church, started the Sanctuary movement, which provided safe haven to the asylum seekers by transporting them across the border to a network of churches and homes, where they were then given shelter.

Heather became actively involved in the movement, and through her participation she began to get involved with church-based work in Central America, making several trips to Guatemala and El Salvador.

In a famous set of trials known as the "Sanctuary Trials," a number of leading figures, including Reverend Fife, were indicted on numerous counts, including "aiding illegal aliens to enter the United States by shielding, harboring, and transporting them." It was about fifteen years after these trials that Fife founded the Samaritans.

On June 27, 2002, just a few months before Chris Simcox published his "call to arms," Reverend Fife published his own call. The Samaritans were being created in order to "save the lives of migrants in the Sonoran Desert," and Fife was looking for volunteers: "We call upon all citizens of good will and people of faith to join us in providing this life-giving aid and hospitality to migrants in need in the desert."

Like Simcox, Fife criticized the government's border policies. But while Simcox indicted the government for failing to do its job to secure the border, Fife accused the government of being "responsible for the mounting toll of suffering, death, and destruction in the desert." "We do this," Fife wrote, "because the current policy and strategy of the Border Patrol (Operation Gatekeeper) deliberately channels the migration of undocumented workers into the most hazardous and deadly regions. The mounting death toll since this immoral strategy was implemented in 1996 is stark evidence of a failed policy that systematically violates human rights."

And like Simcox, Fife argued that patrolling the border, in this instance to "render humanitarian aid," was his right and responsibility: "We believe that respect for human rights, the right to render humanitarian aid under U.S. immigration law, and our ethical responsibility to save human lives demand this of us all." Both spoke of rights, both spoke of duties. Both patrolled the border.

Most of the recruiting documents the Samaritans publish have a section describing civil initiative. The section often begins with a question-and-answer section that starts by posing the question, "Isn't what you do illegal?" The response written is, "No. We work within the law to save lives. We do not engage in civil disobedience, but rather civil initiative."

During his involvement in the Sanctuary movement, Reverend Fife received a telephone call from a lawyer in New York City who was following the movement. Fife says that before the conversation with the lawyer the movement had been framed as a form of civil disobedience.

As he says, "We understood our actions as violating a law which we felt was unjust." The lawyer explained to him, however, that they were not in fact violating any laws. "'Fife,' he said to me, 'you guys are not doing civil disobedience. You aren't arguing for any change to refugee law, what you guys are saying is that refugee laws are fine the way they are; you guys are saying you just want the government to implement those laws, to abide by the refugee laws.'" Fife says that the insight was transformative. He came to a realization that they were not undertaking an act of civil disobedience, they were not asking for any new laws, but for the current laws to be enforced. From that point the Sanctuary movement constructed a concept of political activism known as "civil initiative." As defined by Jim Corbett, one of the founders of the movement, "Civil Initiative is informed by this function: our responsibility for protecting the persecuted must be balanced by our accountability to the legal order. . . . Civil initiative neither evades nor seizes police powers. . . . Civil initiative maintains and extends the rule of law— unlike civil disobedience, which breaks it, and civil obedience, which lets the government break it. The heart of a societal order guided by the rule of law is the principle that the nonviolent protection of basic rights is never illegal."

The Minutemen also say that what they are doing is not illegal. They say that they do not seek to usurp power from the state but rather act as "the eyes and ears of the Border Patrol," as "force multipliers." And just as the Samaritans do, they say they do not seek new laws to be established, but rather for "the laws already in the books to be enforced."

Both are right, and this is the paradox of immigration laws in America. One can be a Samaritan and say that the laws are not being enforced when speaking about providing humanitarian aid to illegal immigrants, and one can be a Minuteman and say that the laws are not being enforced when speaking about stopping illegal immigrants.

So is the difference between asking whether to call the Border Patrol or simply calling the Border Patrol a big or small difference? Is Fred saving lives? Probably not. But neither is Heather. Is Heather stopping illegal immigrants? Probably not. But neither is Fred. That there are differences between these two is certain, but what is also certain is that they, and many of us, imagine this difference as much larger than it is.

The Minutemen often call their actions humanitarian deeds. This terminology can be read as a rhetorical ploy, aimed at gaining sympathy and challenging the media and public conception of them as vigilantes. It is an attempt to frame something that is not "humanitarian" into "humanitarian," regardless of whether the volunteers believe that to be their objective.

But it is more than this. It is important for Fred to give water to José. Just like Heather, it is important to him that he feels like he is saving lives.

The themes of humanitarianism are important to both Heather and Fred, as is the theme of America and being American. Heather tells me, "It is important to do this as an American," just as Fred tells me that he patrols the border "because I am an American."

But throughout their lives, they have been Americans in different ways.

Reflecting on his experience coming home from Vietnam, Fred tells me, "We lost the war because the government didn't want us to win the war. And it wasn't just the government, it was people here, Americans. All those hippies and communists, protesting us while we're getting shot at over there. . . . It's all these folks who are now protesting us. It's the ones calling for amnesty for the illegals. They're the same ones that burned crosses during Vietnam."

Heather protested Vietnam; Fred was a soldier in Vietnam. Heather lives in Arizona. She refers to the militarization of the border as an "invasion." "Look, look, just look at that," she tells me as we see a Border Patrol helicopter flying in the distance, "this is an invasion. I feel like my community is being invaded by the military."

Fred does not live in Arizona. He travels to the border, and he comes for an experience: an experience of war, of soldiering; an experience that connects to the way he has been an American.

The conflict expressed at the border needs to be placed within a larger historical framework. It articulates not just a contemporary conflict, but one whose roots began some thirty years ago when men came home from Vietnam. If José is a target, it is because he represents a larger, and much longer, battle, and a much deeper set of frustrations. The construction of José as an enemy is part of a longer story of conflict—not between Mexicans and Americans, but between Americans and Americans.

The Samaritans

"Somos amigos," "Somos Iglesia," "Neccesita ayuda?" "Tenemos agua," Heather, Nurse Nancy, and Brother David yell out as we hike across a section of the desert. The calls are meant to announce to illegal immigrants that might be hiding in the brush, fearful of any passerby, that the Samaritans are here to help. But as usual, we see no one. Only the usual signs that they had passed by: footprints, discarded backpacks, torn clothing.

Heather decides we ought to try a different location. She knows of some "migrant trails" near the wildlife refuge where "we may have better luck."

We hike back to our truck, an old Jeep that had been donated to the group. Heather takes the wheel. In consideration of his 6-foot-4 frame, Brother John is given the front passenger seat. Nurse Nancy and I ride in the back. Behind us, in the trunk of the car, are over one hundred water bottles, countless pairs of socks, and about fifty packs of food rich in protein and carbohydrates.

The drive to the wildlife refuge is not a very long one, but it is unwieldy, requiring the driver to negotiate numerous rocky hills. As we stutter up the first hill, a pair of binoculars slides down from the dashboard. Brother John bends over from his seat to retrieve them. Heather expresses her gratitude and asks if he can put them in the glove compartment. Brother John does, and as he does I realize that while they always bring binoculars with them, I have never once seen any of the Samaritans use them.

The opening of the car's glove compartment reminds everyone that there is a handheld radio. Brother John takes the radio out of the glove compartment and replaces it with the binoculars.

Just like the Minutemen, the Samaritans often use the radio to listen in to Border Patrol communications. Brother John asks if either Nurse Nancy or I want to take control of the radio. We both remain silent. He turns it on. Heather reminds him that while it is legal to listen in to the communications, if we come across the Border Patrol, he should try to conceal it under the seat because it is frowned upon.

Brother John takes out a binder. The binder contains a number of documents to help while on patrol. These include important phone numbers, maps, a log of "encounters with migrants" as well as one for "encounters with Border Patrol," a list of Spanish words with their English translation, and instructions on basic first aid. Brother John flips to the page that lists the phonetic alphabet as well as the meaning of different acronyms and codes used by the Border Patrol in their radio communications.

The reception is scratchy, but that's not the only thing that keeps Brother John from understanding what is being said. Each time he hears something, he fumbles through the pages of the binder, trying to locate the meaning of the military jargon he hears. "Anyone know what they are saying?" he asks while turning toward Nurse Nancy and me.

The Samaritans use these radios so that they can hear if an illegal immigrant has been apprehended. If an apprehension takes place while they are on patrol, they will often drive to that location to try to give those apprehended some food and water and, as Heather says, "just to be a friendly face in a time of need."

Raising her voice above the scratchy sound of military codes, Heather tells us all to "keep our eyes peeled" as we near the area she was referring to earlier.

Right then we drive past a group of Border Patrol cars parked on the side of the road. "I'm turning around," Heather announces. "It looks like they've just picked someone up."

Heather does a quick U-turn and slows down a few feet behind the set of Border Patrol cars. Three people in handcuffs are being led into the back of one the cars. "Ugh, God. I just feel so awful whenever I see this, no matter how many times I see it, I just feel so awful." She puts the car in park. She suggests it's a good idea for Brother John to get out of the car along with her. Scanning his attire, she says, "Maybe the Border Patrol will be a bit more willing to let us give the migrants food if they see you."

The two get out of the car and walk toward the Border Patrol agents. Nurse Nancy wonders out loud if the Border Patrol will let them "give the migrants some food."

It's less than a minute before Heather and Brother John are back in the car. "God, I hate that," Heather tells us as she puts the car into gear. "You just never know, some agents let us and some don't. They talk about how they have rules that don't allow them to give the migrants outside food, but its all bullshit. If they want to they can." As we drive off we see the faces of one of the illegal immigrants staring wearily out the back of a Border Patrol car. "Ugh, God, just look at that." Heather throws her hands in the air. "It just breaks my heart."

We start the drive back toward the area Heather suggested. Frustrated, she asks Brother John to turn off the radio. "Sorry, I just can't take listening to that thing anymore. I can't stand hearing them talk about these apprehensions."

It's only a few minutes later that we pass by a parked bus used by the Border Patrol to transport apprehended illegal immigrants to Tucson, where they are processed and jailed. Up until 2007 the buses were operated by the Border Patrol. But since 2007, as it had done with the construction of the border fence, the federal government has subcontracted the transport of illegal immigrants to a private company. Different people measure the impacts of this change through the prism of their own particular interests. The government speaks of cutting costs and freeing up agents to patrol the border. Illegal immigrants, whose ambitions and desires lie outside the bus, could care less who is transporting them to jail. For the Samaritans, the impacts are measured in terms of whether they are allowed to give food to illegal immigrants in captivity.

Heather parks the car behind the bus. As before, she and Brother John exit while Nurse Nancy and I stay behind. The two of us watch as the bus doors open and Heather boards while Brother John waves to the driver.

Heather exits the bus. She and Brother John walk toward us with a quick pace. She walks past the driver's-side door and goes straight for the trunk. She opens it up and Nurse Nancy and I turn to look at her, waiting to hear news. "He says we can bring food," Heather tells us, "but we need to be quick about it." She frantically begins to rummage through the supplies lying in the trunk, pushing aside socks and diapers, and picking out packets of food. "It's a full bus," she tell us. Nurse Nancy asks if they need help. Worried the driver might change is mind if he sees the four of us, Heather says it's better if only she and Brother John go.

Nurse Nancy and I wait in the back of the car. We watch Heather and Brother John board the bus and exit a few minutes later. They exchange some words with the driver, nod and wave to him, and make their way toward us.

Nurse Nancy and I ask for details. How many were there? Any women? Children? Were they able to give them food?

Heather sighs. She describes the experience as bittersweet. "It was so sad," she tells us, "seeing all of these poor people in handcuffs like that." Brother John agrees but adds, "At least we were able to give them some food." Heather continues describing the people inside the bus, saying how bad she feels for them, how exhausted and pained they all seemed.

To Brother John's surprise, many of the people on the bus didn't take the food from him. And those who did looked at it and left it unopened. He turns to Heather for an explanation.

She says that it's a "cultural thing." In the places where the illegal immigrants come from, it's considered rude to eat in front of foreigners. She says it's happened many times before. "The thing to do sometimes is to actually open the food up for them and then hand it to them. That way they feel it is OK to start eating." Nurse Nancy explains that one of the other volunteers she went out on patrol with recommends putting the food in a bucket and leaving it on the bus for the illegal immigrants to take themselves instead of passing it out: "Apparently they feel more comfortable that way."

As Heather and Nurse Nancy say this, I am reminded of the Minutemen's own accounts of giving food and water to the illegal immigrants. Minutemen are neither encouraged to give food and water nor discouraged from doing so. "If you want to give them food and water, you can" is what Blowfish tells the volunteers at the patrol briefings. "But just make sure to set it on the ground. Do not have any physical contact with them." While Nurse Nancy's reasoning comes from an idea of cultural sensitivity, Blowfish's is rooted in military strategy and fear. "If you want to give them water, set it on the ground and back away. Don't get too close. They might have a knife on them, and they'll slit your throat, no questions asked," he explains to volunteers.

For the next couple of hours we hike along the desert. Heather, Nurse Nancy, and Brother John make their calls offering help. But we encounter no one. Heather checks her watch. She looks up at the sky. The sun is on its way down. "Well, we should probably call it a day before it gets much darker." Brother John agrees, and we begin our way back. We are driving back not to a camp, but to a church.

The Southside Presbyterian Church is the Samaritans' headquarters. It is where the group stores its supplies—hundreds of socks, shoes, and water bottles. It is where the two cars used for patrols are parked. It is where volunteers meet in the morning before heading out on patrol. And it is also where volunteers meet once a week to discuss group activities.

Every Tuesday the nave of the Southside Presbyterian Church, or simply Southside, as locals call it, is filled not with worshipers but with Samaritans. The nave is a modest circular space with exposed wooden beams overhead and bright wooden pews. Although it is not new, it so well maintained that it has the feel and smell of a new room. It is located a few steps below the ground level of the church, and when you enter it you feel like you have descended underground. And that is just what you are supposed to feel.

The Southside nave is modeled after a Native American prayer room known as a kiva, whose circular design and underground location were meant to promote peaceful reflection and a sense of community and equality among the members, the same ideals that organize a Samaritans meeting.

Walk into a meeting and the first thing you will be struck by is how different it is from Minutemen meetings—not just in what they talk about and how they talk, but in how it looks, how it feels, who is there, and how they are dressed. You'll see women. Not one or two, but a majority of women.[2] You will see a woman standing in front leading the meeting. You will see no camouflage. The Samaritans meetings have the feel of a cross between a religious meeting and an organizational meeting. One thing they are decidedly not is a military briefing.

Each meeting is lead by a facilitator, usually alternating between members of a subgroup of experienced volunteers, the majority of whom are women. As the title indicates, the facilitator's role is to aid in running the conversation. In meetings this means remaining objective, raising questions when needed, and making sure there is enough time to let everyone speak who wants to speak. Volunteers judge the performance of the facilitators based on their capacity to follow these expectations, and the majority say that Meghan, a middle school teacher, fulfills the role of facilitator best. "She never imposes her own opinions," a volunteer explains to me.

Meghan has short, fluffy gray hair. She is soft-spoken and maintains a calm demeanor throughout meetings, even when tensions rise. Very rarely do members speak over each other, but when they do, Meghan is known to put her hand out in a calming gesture and remind everyone to wait their turn before they speak.

The meeting is about to begin. Meghan stands in the middle of the circular nave and welcomes everyone. Next to her is a dry-erase board. As with every meeting, she begins by asking for a moment of silence. "Let us take a moment to collect our thoughts," she tells us, "and pray for our brothers and sisters who are crossing the desert." Everyone bows their heads. The silence lasts for about thirty seconds. With my head down I almost instinctively wait for the sound of a military drumbeat, as happens in the Minutemen camp when heads are bowed. But this ritual is much different; this is a religious moment, not a military moment.

After the pause Meghan asks that we introduce ourselves. One by one members go around the room giving their names. For the most part, everyone knows everyone else, and the introductions are less about specifying who is in the room and more about establishing a friendly atmosphere. It is this atmosphere of compassion and care that both defines the organizational meetings and is the atmosphere the group seeks to bring to the border during their patrols.

When the Samaritans were first established, they were actually called Samaritan Patrol. Just as the Minutemen changed their name from the Tombstone Militia to the Minutemen, so too did the Samaritans change their name, dropping the "patrol" from their title. The Samaritans wanted to distance themselves from language that aligned their actions with any kind of militarism. Just as the Minutemen seek to establish a connection between what they do and the Minutemen from the Revolutionary War, so too the Samaritans, by using that name, seek to establish a connection between what they are doing and the biblical Israeli tribe of the same name, known for their generosity and hospitality toward those in need.

Meghan lists the next agenda item as "Sister Organizations," referring to other groups, most prominently No More Deaths and Humane

Borders, that seek to provide humanitarian assistance along with border. The naming of these as sister organizations at once defines them as partners and establishes a gendered idea of what the relations between them is, and what it is that they each do on the border. While the Minutemen camp presents itself as a masculine space, the Samaritans' organizational meeting present itself as a feminine one.

Meghan finishes writing down the standard agenda items. Following "Sister Organizations" is "Old Business." She then turns to the room and asks if there is anything else she should add to the list. People raise their hands offering additional agenda items they would like to see covered, and Meghan promptly writes them down.

While Meghan is in charge of the meeting, there is no real hierarchy. Indeed, everyone inside the church is an equal when it comes to having their opinions heard and counted. Quite the opposite of a chain of command, the organizational meetings are run as a participatory democracy. When decisions are made, they are put to a vote, with the aim of achieving consensus. Members signal their approval or disapproval through various hand gestures, from wiggling their fingers to waving their hands. Put simply, these meetings are not military briefings— neither in their content nor in their form. The meetings last for an hour and a half, and then they end. They are not conversations about strategies and details about the patrol that will follow. The Samaritans have no such conversations before they go out on patrol.

Unlike the Minutemen, the Samaritans patrol the border mainly by walking through the desert. They do not position themselves on lawn chairs, standing post as a coordinated group in military formation. In some ways their walks through the desert are similar to those taken by the Minutemen's Search and Rescue Team. But while the Samaritans speak of them as "hikes," the Minutemen speak of them as "recon work." While the Samaritans describe walking through the desert as reliving "the migrant experience," the Minutemen describe walking through the desert as reliving their experiences in Vietnam.

When I ask Brother John how he came to join the Samaritans, he tells me it was a result of "taking a long walk." He explains that he means this both metaphorically and literally. "I was a mess. I was in my early twenties and basically living on the streets of Kansas City. One day I decided to take a trip from Kansas City to Chicago by foot. I hitchhiked every now and then, but I mostly hiked the whole way." In Chicago Brother John lived and worked at a homeless shelter, and he says this was a "transformative experience": "I decided it was my calling. To be involved with helping those in need."

The trope of walking as a religious experience of pilgrimage is an important one in the Samaritans' understanding of what they are doing when they "hike in the desert." They talk about the importance of physically walking through the desert and experiencing what the "migrants experience." They say that such an experience helps one understand what the "migrants go through." In this way they see the hikes as being transformative moments, as influencing their own sense of self. These hikes are like religious pilgrimages.

Heather is clearly the one in charge of our group, but there is nothing remotely close to the idea of a line leader. Indeed, the notion of a chain of command with its hierarchy based on previous military experience is nowhere to be found among the Samaritans. If Heather is in charge, it has to do as much with the fact that she is the most experienced among the four of us as it does with her eager personality. Her requests come across as favors, not orders; following them is a discretionary act based on willingness, and not following them doesn't carry consequences beyond dirty looks or expressed frustrations.

For the Minutemen a key part of the meaning of patrols comes from their camp. The Samaritans have no such camp. While the Minutemen hold their meetings under a canopy with a strict hierarchical order, the Samaritans hold their meetings in a church. The Samaritans don't patrol at night because it is dangerous; the Minutemen prove themselves by patrolling at night.

Like the Minutemen, the Samaritans have handheld radios they use on patrol. But the truth is they don't know how to use them. Not just that, no one really wants to hold them. The Minutemen fight over these radios. The practical efficacy of the radios on their politics is not so great, but the impact on giving meaning and making the act of patrol meaningful is enormous.

Same acts, done differently. And that's where the meaning comes from. Is this the result of different ideas about immigration? Yes and no. That's part of it. But it is more about different ways of being in the world—different ways that the patrols fit into who they are and who they have been their entire lives.

Heather's Story: Who Do You Think We Are, the Minutemen?

We were on our way back to truck. He was sort of just wandering around the truck, probably waiting for someone to find him.

His name was Julio. He was twenty-four and had been walking alone for four days. He said that he had sprained his ankle and that he couldn't keep up with the group he was crossing with.

He was from Veracruz and had a wife and two kids back home. He was coming to work in Chicago, where he said he had some family.

We gave him some food and water, and Nurse Nancy took a look at his feet. They were in awful shape. I mean they had these giant blisters all over. And so we bandaged him up and got him a new pair of socks and shoes.

He was actually a really funny guy. He kept asking us if we could give him a ride and we explained that we couldn't do that, and he kept saying that he was a really small guy and could fit into the trunk.

He said he couldn't walk anymore. He said he was too tired and that his feet were hurting too much.

We asked him if he wanted us to call the Border Patrol and he said yes.

It was so annoying. I got transferred like six different times, one agent putting me on hold, then another. Finally I got through to someone and they said they would send an agent to come pick him up.

We must have waited for like four hours. I mean when we first saw him it was light out and by the time the agent came it was totally dark.

Anyway, he was really funny. He kept making jokes about how the Border Patrol doesn't want him.

Anyway, finally the agent comes. He was actually relatively nice. I mean he treated Julio pretty well; he was gentle with him and helped him into the back of the truck. I mean you hate to see it, but at least he wasn't being a total asshole.

But then it was so crazy, the agent rolls down his window and he says, "Good job." Good job?! I mean who did he think we were, the Minutemen?

ANDREA DYLEWSKI

Belonging in America

||||||||||||||||||||||||||||||||||||||||

As CHRIS SIMCOX TELLS IT, shortly after 9/11 he left his job as a kindergarten teacher in a private school outside Los Angeles, where he also ran a small educational consulting company, to go on a forty-day solitary camping trip in Arizona's Organ Pipe Cactus National Park. The trip, Simcox says, was a necessary respite for him at a moment when he was overwhelmed by anger and grief at what had befallen his country. While meditating in the park, Chris says he witnessed "five groups of paramilitary drug dealers just driving caravans of vehicles right into this country." After alerting the park services and receiving a cavalier response, he had what he describes as an "awakening," and the idea was born in his mind to start a citizen's group whose aim would be to protect the borders of the United States from "illegal invasion."

While Chris often tells people, and especially media outlets, the creation story of the Minutemen as a biblical tale of one man's inspiration and awakening, the actual story of the group's emergence, as well as Chris's own motivations and role in forming it, are both much more complex and much less charismatic. This was not the result of individual inspiration; it was a combination of personal needs and social forces.

In the months leading up to 9/11, Chris was going through a nasty divorce with his ex-wife. By all accounts he was an emotional wreck. His wife was seeking a restraining order, and on the evening of September 11 Chris left a message on her voice mail: "I will not speak to my son or anyone again until you can recite the . . . at least begin the preamble of the Constitution. . . . I am dead serious, that's how much of an American I am."[1] On September 13 he left another message explaining that the next time he saw his son, "I will begin teaching him the art of protecting himself with weapons. . . . I purchased another gun, I've applied for another one, I have more than a few weapons, and I intend to begin teaching my son how to use them. . . . I will begin inundating my son with new frames of mind. . . . I must teach my son how to protect himself."[2] While the comments focused on molding his son into a new person, they were equally directed toward Chris himself, outlining a self-fashioning he would undertake over the course of the following years.

Chris decided to leave Los Angeles. He was going to enlist in the military, but there was a problem: the military wouldn't take him. He was too old. He found an alternative: he was going to Arizona to join the Border Patrol. "I'm packing up," he told his son, "I'm going to go down to the Mexican border and I'm signing up for the government for Border Patrol . . . and I'm going to become a Border Patrol officer for the government . . . to protect the borders of the country that I love." Feeling guilty about abandoning his son, Chris continued, "I'm not walking away from you . . . I'm going to help my country . . . you got it . . . the military wouldn't take me . . . because of my health and because of my age . . . the Border Patrol will take me . . . they're hiring and I'm going down there."[3]

Tombstone, "the town too tough to die," has a population of just over a thousand and exists in the American imagination as the preeminent symbol of the old "Wild West." It was in and near Tombstone that cowboys waged a continuous fight against northern capitalists and immigrant miners who were becoming a dominant presence in the town. This tension famously exploded on October 26, 1881, with the gunfight at the O.K. Corral, which involved some of the most notorious figures of the Old West, including Wyatt Earp, Doc Holliday, and Billy Claiborne.

When the mines were depleted, Tombstone turned into a major tourist attraction, constructed as a fantasy, living off its mythologized past. In 1961 the government designated it a National Historic District that boasts "one of the best preserved specimens of the rugged frontier town of the 1870s and '80s." Modern-day Tombstone, where towering images of the O.K. Corral form the town's only semblance of a skyline and almost all street life is motivated by daily re-creations of the gunfight on one of the many purposefully unpaved streets cordoned off from vehicle traffic, is dominated by this past.

The frontier has always played a privileged role in the American mythology of nation building. Writing in the nineteenth century, Frederick Jackson Turner famously located the heart of the American identity in the frontier, specifically in the experience of encountering and taming the uncivilized world. Turner's fear was that at the dawn of the twentieth century, with American expansion reaching its end point, frontiers were running out, and so too the American experience. But it is in Tombstone, and southern Arizona more generally, in the twenty-first century that the frontier has been reborn. Here Chris Simcox also hoped to be reborn.

But the Border Patrol wouldn't take Chris either. Much as he talks about wanting to "shame the state," and much as we see him, through the lens of vigilantism, as someone wanting to circumvent the state, his first inclination was to join the state. But the state rejected him. Part of Chris's actual story of establishing the Minutemen is fundamentally one of being excluded from participating as a formal agent of the state. He didn't want to start a militia; it was a last resort. And in this there is great similarity between Chris Simcox and the other volunteers: it is not their ideology that leads them to establish their camp, it is their age.

Luckily for Chris, a one-time budding actor, the daily reenactments of the gunfight at the O.K. Corral were in need of actors. For his first year in Tombstone, he made a living by playing Wyatt Earp. And it was during that time that he met a former Border Patrol officer who had taken to patrolling the border with a group of other men. Chris was all too eager to join.

Though Chris undoubtedly played a key role in the founding and success of the Minutemen, like most social movements, the banding together of a group of citizens to patrol the U.S.-Mexico border in order to apprehend illegal immigrants was not the result of a single individual's ideas or actions.

When Chris moved to Arizona in November 2001, he knowingly entered a landscape filled with a burgeoning movement of private citizens undertaking patrolling operations; the phenomenon of citizens patrolling the border had a history, and a particularly keen one in southern Arizona.[4] In fact, in his original call to arms Simcox made comparisons with previous patrol groups, writing that unlike other groups, his organization would patrol "actually on the border, not 25 miles from the border, as is now the practice."

When I met Chris Simcox for lunch in the summer of 2008, he had gone through a lifetime of change since we had first met three years earlier. He had remarried, for the third time. His Greek American wife, who came from a very well-to-do family, had recently given birth to their first child, and they were living in Scottsdale, a bastion of upper-middle-class refugees from nearby Phoenix. Most important, Chris had gone from being the head of the Tombstone Militia, a relatively unknown group, to being the president of the Minutemen Civil Defense Corps, a social movement that had gained a strong foothold in the heart of American politics and public debate. He was now challenging Arizona Senator John McCain for his seat in the Senate. And as Simcox changed, so too did the Minutemen. Organizational money and energy were being redirected from the patrols to the campaign. But while Simcox embraced all these changes, the rank and file met them with resentment. The changes were good for Simcox, but they were bad for the volunteers. While Chris had found a new place in America, the volunteers were left still searching for theirs.

Filled with gated communities that go by names like Pleasant Hills and Parkview Terrace, Scottsdale is a long way from Tombstone, where Chris first began his project to defend America. He suggests he is having a difficult time adjusting to life in Scottsdale. He moved there primarily as a compromise with his wife: "She likes the shops and the cafes, but you know, suburbs just aren't my thing, I'm more of the rugged individual." But although Chris likes to present himself as someone suited for the contours of the "Wild West," the truth is that Scottsdale is where he is at home. As Tombstone locals used to say when he first arrived in town as an immigrant from Los Angeles, "he's more of a surfer dude than a rancher dude."

While Tombstone is stuck in the past, Scottsdale has moved on. From the mid-1990s Scottsdale has been at the epicenter of Arizona's economic boom. It saw its population soar between 1990 and 2008, from 140,000 to just under 250,000. Most residents are recent émigrés from Phoenix, seeking to escape that city's diversity, crime, and traffic. Scottsdale is 90 percent white, and the median family income is around $75,000. Filled with high-end shops, cafes, and numerous bars and restaurants with international cuisine, Scottsdale has been described in the *New York Times* as "a desert version of Miami's South Beach."[5]

Like the neighborhood where he now lives, Chris has moved on as well. He is more manicured; the scruffy and unkempt hair is long gone, and the formerly gaunt face is now filled out. He drives a brand new luxury car. He seems to be doing well, financially and emotionally. He seems to be embracing his new life. But he is no longer a Minuteman. Not in the sense that the rank-and-file volunteers understand what it means to be a Minuteman.

Chris tells me that with me, he can talk about things that the volunteers wouldn't "understand." "I can say things to you which I can't to them because they just don't get it." Recalling the day he kicked me out of the camp and considered me a "mole," I push him to tell me more. "Me and you," he says, "we are both educators. A lot of these guys, they can't see the forest for the trees. From the beginning I knew I couldn't catch every immigrant coming across the border. A lot of them, all they care about are the apprehensions, but they don't get it. They don't get how it works. They don't understand the impact. They don't get what this is about." There is a lot of truth in what he says. But while he claims that the volunteers "don't get what this is about," the truth is, it is Chris who doesn't exactly get "what this is all about." And neither do we.

There are many ways we can approach trying to understand the Minutemen. As I have argued throughout this book, the dominant narrative about these men, the one that sees their presence on the border as a consequence of a set of anti-immigrant beliefs, the one that seeks to understand their patrols by focusing on what they do when they encounter illegal immigrants, won't get us very far; it won't get us to the camp, but that is where we need to go to understand what being a Minuteman is all about, and that is where I want to go one last time.

By the start of 2007, many things had changed with the Minutemen. They were changes that marked the group's success, but also its impending downfall. Donations were pouring in to support the "Israeli fence"; Simcox was traveling across the country giving lectures; he hired the consulting firm Denier Associates to manage finances and public relations; he even started a political action committee. But this was not what the volunteers had signed up for; this was not what being a Minuteman was about.

Members began to feel alienated from the organization, an organization that was increasingly focusing on gaining a foothold in public office and not on patrolling the border. They started to question their affiliation. The Minutemen started to look more and more like the institutions they were fighting against: the government, the politicians. And then the big blow came.

In the middle of the summer of 2007, Chris Simcox got into a heated argument with Blowfish. It is not clear exactly what the argument was about. But what is clear is that Simcox told Blowfish to leave the camp; while he said Blowfish was being "suspended," the volunteers said Blowfish was being asked to "stand down." By some accounts the suspension was for one week, by others one month. But it didn't matter— Blowfish would never return. And Simcox had messed with the wrong Minuteman.

Chris Simcox and Blowfish represent two very different elements in the Minutemen organization: Simcox is the ideologue and Blowfish is the soldier. While the practices that define Simcox involve giving lectures, the ones that define Blowfish involve patrolling the border. And in this sense, for the volunteers, it is not Simcox who represents the Minutemen, but Blowfish, and his dismissal caused a backlash.

The admiration for Blowfish came pouring in: "He ran the lines like Swiss watches," "he was tough, but he protected your ass." People talked about the "low morale" in the camp. They started talking about Chris's "ego." Members began circulating a petition calling for the reinstatement of Blowfish, and they called for a meeting with Simcox. The petition voiced anger at Blowfish's treatment and described him as "exemplary in his loyalty and dedication" and someone who "has been a consistent leader in border operations and is the most trusted of all line leaders." The petition was sent out, along with the request for a meeting with Simcox in which members stated that while Simcox should remain the head of the organization, he should not have any authority over what happens at the camp. That, after all, is what mattered to these men. Simcox responded by threatening to suspend more members, calling the petition "illegal."

Suddenly it was not the illegal immigrant who was the enemy, but Chris Simcox. The fight against Chris became an expression of patriotism. As one Minutemen wrote to fellow volunteers, "We would be less than Patriots if we were to sit back and allow this kind of behavior go un-answered. . . . Just because a few people hold a piece of paper saying they own some half assed corporation, does not mean they own the MOVEMENT. We the PEOPLE own this movement, just as we the PEOPLE own the United States of America. To try and hold PATRIOTS down, to control what they have to say, to hide in the shadows behind lawyers and cheap suits is NOT America. This is NOT what the Cause is about."

One by one, members started to resign. The reasons were variations on the same theme: a sense of alienation; a sense that the movement had stopped being about the camp and the patrols. As one volunteer put it in his resignation letter, "After spending 30 years in the Corps and thinking I found an outfit like the Minutemen that would fill a void in where America is heading . . . I then find that the carpet has been pulled out from under me." The Minutemen splintered, and a second group was formed. But things would never be the same. The men had lost something very important. "Border watches have becomes like 'old home week,'" Ernest, who had been to every single patrol muster, explained, "renewing acquaintances, visiting with old comrades, having fun, being appreciated by the local residents. . . . Should the border watches be discontinued, I would be deeply saddened."

Have the Minutemen been a success or a failure? It depends on how we understand what this group is about. If we focus on Chris Simcox and think of politics as votes and seats in Congress, the group is a success story. Even though Chris was never elected to office, the group gained a strong foothold in American politics and in very important ways became the stimulus for the Tea Party movement that emerged in 2010. But for the volunteers, the success of the Minutemen is not about gaining a foothold in Congress. It is not about immigration policy. It is not about "ideology," it is about the practice of politics. And to understand the rank-and-file Minutemen, focusing on Chris Simcox would be a mistake.

If you want to figure out the Minutemen "ideology" you can talk to Chris. You can interview him and he'll tell you what the Minutemen's "politics" are. He is the voice of the group. But he is not a Minuteman— not in the sense that the volunteers are, not in the sense that they want to be, not in the sense that they were hoping to be by coming down to the border. You don't need to travel to the border to be Chris Simcox, but you do need to travel to the border to be a Minuteman.

What role does the U.S.-Mexico border play in the Minutemen's lives? For them, the border has become a resource for restoring conditions of life that they have struggled to maintain: soldiering, securing the nation, protecting family members, and establishing masculine camaraderie. By patrolling the border they escape the sense of meaninglessness that defines their current lives as aging veterans and find a renewed sense of meaning and purpose.

Afterword to the Paperback Edition
||||||||||||||||||||||||||||||||||||||||||||

In October of 2008, I left the Minutemen campground for the last time. As I was packing, Stanley, better known by his handle "Mussels," told me about an exchange that he and a fellow Minuteman had had while hiking in a wildlife refuge the previous day. As they were returning to their cars after their hike, a resident of the Valley confronted them. Mussels recounted, "She was yelling at us, calling us racists, telling us that the illegals are just looking for some work, just trying to feed their families and that we have no right to be doing what we are doing." While the other Minuteman "started going back and forth with the woman, debating the whole immigration issue," Mussels said he just remained quiet because he has learned over time not to "bother with people like that," since "I'm not going to change what she thinks, and she is not going to change what I think."

Although he remained silent during the encounter, Mussels was clearly bothered by the criticisms that were leveled against him. After all, like all the other Minutemen I had met on the border, he did not consider himself a racist. Moreover, Mussels thought that he was being morally virtuous by traveling all the way from his hometown of New Hampshire to Southern Arizona to patrol the border. And while being a called a racist wasn't pleasant for him, Mussels had developed a fairly robust armor of disregard against such claims—indeed against most criticisms of his membership with the Minutemen. There was something else that bothered Mussels though. Beyond the criticisms against him, he was troubled by the fact that he simply could not comprehend how two people could hold such different opinions about immigration. Even more, Mussels could not comprehend how someone who lived on the border, in the very community he was there to protect, would not embrace his presence and affirm his actions and beliefs.

To that point, over the course of my three years spending time with the Minutemen, Mussels, like most other volunteers, had treated me as a student, as someone to educate, and not as someone to be educated by. But as I was saying goodbye, and explaining to him that this was most likely my last research trip, the script was reversed: Mussels looked to me for explanation. "You're the Sociologist! Explain it to me Harel, because I just can't wrap my head around it. How is it that this person, who lives in a community that has illegals coming through on a daily basis, that has trash all over the place because of the illegals, that has to live in fear because of the illegals, how is it that she can think the way she does? How is that two people can think so differently about the same thing?"

As I write in January 2017, days after the inauguration of Donald Trump, a president whose victory was celebrated by some Americans as enthusiastically as it was lamented by others, the chasm between people like Mussels and the woman he encountered on the border appears to be larger than ever. Moreover, the project of keeping out undesirable foreigners who are believed to represent a variety of cultural and economic threats has resurfaced with a vengeance. And while a resurgent desire for walls appears particularly pronounced in the United States, in which a president was elected under the promise of building a "great wall" between the United States and Mexico as part of a larger project to "protect the homeland," this is not simply an American story, but rather a global one.

Since the publication of *Waiting for José*, borders across the world have been fortified and, in some cases, built for the very first time. Hungary has built a wall along its border with Serbia and is far along in the process of building one along its border with Romania; Spain, a key point of entry for immigrants from Northern Africa into the European Union has walled off its borders to the South; Saudi Arabia has built a wall with Yemen; Israel with Egypt; Egypt with Morocco; India with Bangladesh; Russia with Estonia; Norway with Russia; Britain with France; and on, and on. And increasingly, civilians are participating in this project of building and policing borders: armed Bulgarian civilians are patrolling their country's border with Turkey, while South African farmers are patrolling their borders with Zimbabwe. All of these remind us how profound the discourse and infrastructure of borders and border militarization is around the world. They remind us that while technological changes and financial deregulations have increased certain kinds of mobility, for each new institution meant to enable movement there seems to be one meant to prohibit it. For every NAFTA, there is a Border Patrol; for every Schengen, a Frontex. And for every person who is critical of the project of militarizing borders there is a Minuteman; a person who was patrolling the border a decade ago and celebrating Trump's inauguration a few days ago. Within this contemporary and global context of heightened divisions and increased fortifications, the question Mussels posed to me nearly a decade ago seems as relevant as ever before.

Walls and borders have powerful consequences at the level of large-scale geo-politics. But they also have powerful consequences in terms of small scale interpersonal relationships: they make it so that people like Mussels do not have to see or encounter the immigrant. Mussels's search for understanding of the woman he encountered, a local white citizen, appears to be genuine, still, in my years of knowing him he never once declared that he wanted to speak to an illegal immigrant to learn from them about their reasons for crossing the border. Indeed, understanding those who were crossing the border requires having precisely the kind of interactions and encounters which Mussels himself was on the border to deny. It is the border, in both its material and symbolic form, that same border which Mussels was in Southern Arizona volunteering to help fortify and defend, which denies Mussels and in fact protects him from the kind of understanding of, and relationship with, those he fears that he needs to have.

It is not that Mussels does not seek knowledge of the people coming across the border. He does. And his position on the border, both literally and figuratively, is supported by a certain kind of knowledge and understanding of the immigrant. Immigration policies are developed by raising a whole host of questions about immigrants: Who are they? What are their thoughts? What are their desires? Embedded in ethno-nationalist ambitions and fears, these questions are often answered in ways that point to those outside our borders as being responsible for a wide range of internal problems: economic, cultural, social. Framed around this cadre of ills, the immigrant is seen as contaminating the nation in both symbolic and material ways, and the danger they pose is conceptualized as being at once both very abstract and very real. Consider the following exchange between two Minutemen waiting to go out on patrol:

"I live in D.C., and let me tell you," the first one says, "that place has gone to shit. Everyone speaks Spanish."

"You should be careful eating at restaurants in those cities," the second responds, transitioning from the cultural contamination (they speak Spanish) into a physical one, "you don't know what diseases those illegals working in the kitchen are carrying. You should get your meat cooked well done." Such ostensible knowledge about the immigrant, such a sense of certainty about who they are, provides an important legitimacy to the project of militarizing borders – both to elected officials who pass legislation and to civilians who patrol the border with groups like the Minutemen. But to truly understand the amazing power contained within the epistemic logic of borders, it is necessary to see how this sense of certainty about the immigrant is coupled by its opposite: a deep anxiety about their identity. "We don't know who they are," Minutemen president Chris Simcox often told me, in words echoed by Donald Trump, "we just don't know. That's why we need to better vet them." It is in the concept of "vetting" that the epistemic logic of borders finds its ultimate expression, where knowledge about the immigrant and uncertainty about the immigrant unite and make the quest for knowledge about the immigrant inextricable from the quest for surveillance of the immigrant. Knowledge becomes surveillance, surveillance becomes knowledge.

One of the key organizing ideas behind *Waiting for José* was to shift this gaze inward. Instead of focusing on "them," on those on the other side of the border, we would do well to focus on ourselves and our communities: what does the border say about *us*? What is it that someone like Mussels is doing and wanting at the border? What kinds of relationships does the border support, and what kinds of relationships does it deny?

There are significant ideological differences between people like Mussels and the woman who criticized him. Indeed, part of the answer to his question about how two people can think so differently "about the same thing" is to recognize the extent to which they are not in fact thinking about the same thing. Where Mussels sees an "illegal" the local resident sees an "undocumented migrant." Such is the power of ideology. But as I argue in *Waiting for José*, ideological commitments are only one part of what differentiates Mussels from "liberal" America. Beyond examining Mussels's beliefs about immigration, we need to understand his biography and life experiences. In part, these will help us to better understand how his beliefs were developed, but even more, they will help us understand the kinds of social relationships and ways of being in the world, which Mussels seeks, and which the border offers and affirms.

It matters, for example, that unlike this local resident, Mussels was not from the Valley. It matters, that the previous time Mussels, a now-aging military veteran, was in Southern Arizona was when he was stationed at the Fort Huachuca army base. It matters that while Mussels now travels around the country in his RV, up until a few years ago his only experience of the world outside the rural town where he grew up was through the military. It matters that Mussels had very little actual face-to-face experience with the "illegals" whom he feared so much that he took it upon himself to protect the local resident from them. It matters, most of all, that the experiences Mussels did have, the ways of understanding and responding to the world that he did carry with him all the way from New Hampshire, indeed, all the way from his time in Korea, was that of a soldier. And the border, defined then and even more so today, as a battlefield to be secured through military might, provided a stage on which to engage in the kinds of militarized activities and relationships for which Mussels was searching. Indeed, as *Waiting for José* shows, the border and its role in American identity is constitutive of, and at the same time constituted by, a set of practices and experiences by which white, working-class men have found community and purpose—and an otherwise elusive sense of entitlement—through military service. Through the lens of soldiering and of protecting the "homeland," the border is invested with meaning that goes beyond the racist ideological tropes that also inform its militarization.

Defending the border then, holds enormous appeal. As mentioned before, part of its appeal comes from the idea that keeping certain unwanted foreigners out will solve a host of problems. Social scientists have done well to counter this account by documenting the positive impacts of immigrants, legal and illegal, whether in terms of economic gains (Borjas 1995) or social ones (Bloemraad et al. 2008). They have established that within this recent focus on the need to militarize the border, the number of illegal immigrants crossing the border over the past decade has actually been extremely low, and that in fact, rather than stopping illegal immigrants from crossing the border, the increased militarization has had the counter-effect of stopping those already inside America from returning home (Massey and Pren 2012). The articulation and circulation of such facts is important. But to think that all that Mussels misses are these facts, is to miss something crucial about the significance of borders, and what it is that draws people like Mussels to patrol them. What matters for Mussels is not the "practical" impacts of his patrols, that is, the extent to which his presence on the border helps stop illegal immigrants. Yes, illegal immigration matters to the Minutemen, but it matters first and foremost because through it these men have created a culture, a camp, a set of heroes, a set of enemies, an entire social world, through which their past is extended, resurrected, and in the case of some, even invented. Illegal immigration matters, the war on terror matters, but they matter because they have enabled a world to get created down on the border. And if we are to understand the appeal of the militarized border, we need to understand the appeal of this militarized world.

For the most part, Mussels and the other Minutemen found what they were searching for on the border. They found a lost sense of camaraderie and masculinity that reminded them of their days fighting in Korea, Vietnam, or Iraq. But at times, they found something that they were not searching for: a sympathetic understanding of the illegal immigrant.

Except for a couple of passing mentions, face-to-face encounters with illegal immigrants are almost non-existent in *Waiting for José*. This is because they rarely happened. And, for the most part, even though they rarely happened, people like Mussels still found their experiences on the border rewarding. This is because what sustained the experience and gave it meaning was the process of patrolling and the interactions and social life of the Minutemen camp. When the Minutemen did encounter illegal immigrants, it was usually not a face-to-face encounter. Instead the encounter took place through other mediums and objects: footprints in the desert; clothes hanging in mesquite trees; helicopters flying overhead. Armed with their ideological frameworks and militarized way of understanding the world, they read these signs as confirmation that the people coming across the border were dangerous and that they needed to be stopped. But it was when they came face-to-face with the enemy, that their worldviews and practices were most threatened.

While abstractly, the Minutemen could speak about drug runners and rapists, when they talked about the people they actually encountered in person, the accounts were radically different. They spoke of people who were exhausted, who were hungry, who were thirsty. Sometimes, they even spoke about their own fears and apprehensions being challenged. One of the more powerful accounts of this came from a volunteer from Virginia named John:

> There was one time I nearly pulled out my gun. I was out on patrol with my wife, it was night time, it was real dark and all. We're standing post, and I see some guy all alone about fifty feet ahead of us. I say to my wife, 'Hey look over there, you see that?' And she looks and she says, 'yeah, is that an illegal?' Well he's not moving for about twenty minutes or so and finally we decide to see if it's an illegal. So I try to call him over, I say 'Aqui, Aqui' or maybe it was 'Agua, Agua', whatever little Spanish I know.
>
> The guy was shivering. I mean it was a real cold night, so we gave him our blanket and some food. My wife went to the truck and got him a jacket. And he sat with us for about thirty minutes and I'm looking at this guy just shivering, I mean he couldn't control it. I just felt terrible for him.
>
> At one point he reached for his back pocket. I reached for my gun. I thought maybe he was going to take out a knife or something, but he took out his wallet. And he shows us all these I.D.'s he had on him. I didn't really look at them, but now I really wish I did to see what they were, to see who he was.

A few days after relaying this incident to me, John and I were gathered with some other Minutemen. When the conversation turned, as it often did, to the drug runners and terrorists that were coming through the border, John commented that, "so far the only people I've come across seem like good people who are just desperate." I had heard variations of John's comment a few times, and every time, I had heard the following denouncements, "yeah, well, it only takes one of them," and "sure, we all feel bad for them, but if you want to come here you need to do it legally."

Any account of the above encounter and its potentially transformative powers needs to reckon with the fact that John and his wife continued to patrol the border in the days and weeks after this incident. It needs to contend with the fact that even though John recognizes his impulse to reach for his gun was proven to be based on mistaken assumptions, the next time he went on patrol, he still took his gun. And although I have not spoken to him since, I am very confident that John and his wife would have enthusiastically cast their ballots for Donald Trump. Still, there is a moment, a kernel of radical potential that I believe should be recognized. A moment in which the abstract "illegal" turns into the real person. The moment at which the "illegal" turns into a "desperate" person shivering in the middle of the desert. But the moment is a fleeting one, quickly repaired and reframed in a way that reaffirms that these people are dangerous and that the Minutemen are protecting the homeland. Indeed, while moments of sympathy do perhaps have some transformative potential, it is likewise necessary to recognize that the Minutemen did not simply lack sympathy for the people coming across the border. If we are going to fully recognize and come to terms with the power of the border, we need to come to terms with the fact that even though the Minutemen sometimes felt sympathy they still engaged in patrolling the border.

Sympathy could perhaps lead the Minutemen to alter their actions. But there is a difference between the kind of sympathy I saw the Minutemen express and the real level of respect and dialogue that is a requirement for change. These days, we see Donald Trump hoist the mantle of sympathy often. For example, he talks about the broken "inner cities" but his sympathy for victims of crime in Chicago is framed in ways that promote the use of military power (sending federal policing agents to Chicago), in order to ostensibly save these communities from themselves. Not only is sympathy not enough, we need to recognize the ways in which sympathy can be mobilized to further the projects of militarization and wall-building. We need to recognize that sympathy is not opposed to, but compatible with directing violence against those same communities for which one claims to be sympathetic. The Minutemen often spoke of women being raped while making their way across the border, of people being forced into crossing the border because of drug gangs, of good people shivering in the desert as they try to make a better life. But unfortunately, this sympathy towards the other does not materialize in building relationships, but rather in building walls.

January 2016

References to the afterword

Bloemraad, I., A. Korteweg, and G. Yurdakul. 2008. "Citizenship and Immigration: Multiculturalism, Assimilation, and Challenges to the Nation-State. *Annual Review of Sociology* 34: 153-179.

Borjas, George. 1995. "The Economic Benefits from Immigration," *Journal of Economic Perspectives* 9 (2): 3-22.

Massey D., and K. Pren. 2012. "Unintended Consequences of U.S. Immigration Policy: Explaining the Post – 1965 Surge from Latin America," *Population and Development Review* 38: 1–29.

Appendix: A Note on Methodology
IIIIIIIIIIIIIIIIIIIIIIIIIIIIIIIIIIIIIIIIIII

THIS BOOK BEGINS WITH A SIMPLE QUESTION: what motivates people to participate in social movements? It is a question that has stood at the heart of social science research for more than a century, prompting a variety of approaches and revealing transformations in the way that scholars think about political identity and participation.

In many ways the book follows the recent work of scholars of the New Social Movements, who have called for a return to an older way of making sense of social movement participation in which the focus is not on organizational dynamics, as most scholarship on social movements has been since the 1970s, but rather on the identities of participants.[1] However, while I follow this call, in this book I rethink what it means to understand the identity of social movement participants and how we should go about understanding them.

One approach to the question of what motivates people to participate in social movements, which gained prominence in the 1950s, is to focus on the state of mind of the individual participants. This includes taking account of the participants' grievances, personality, emotions, and, most decisively, beliefs and opinions. An important argument is built into this approach: explaining differences in social movement participation requires explaining differences in political attitudes and beliefs. Social movements are defined first and foremost in terms of the set of opinions and beliefs they are organized around, and to understand the participants entails understanding why they hold these opinions while those who do not participate in the movement do not. Social movements and their participants can then be partitioned into "right-wing" or "left-wing" movements, depending on the set of beliefs their members hold.[2]

Starting towards the end of the 1970s, a new generation of scholars introduced a radically different approach known as Resource Mobilization theory, organized in large part as a critique of the idea that beliefs and attitudes are the driving force determining movement participation.[3]

Resource Mobilization scholars have shown that while many people in a society share beliefs and attitudes, it is only a small subset of these who join a movement. Explaining participation therefore becomes a matter of more than simply accounting for differences in beliefs. For Resource Mobilization scholars there is another set of forces at work, ones that do not originate in the individual but rather in the movement itself, in how it is organized and how it works to mobilize potential members.

In this way Resource Mobilization scholars shift the focus from looking at individual participants to considering a social movement's organization. Understanding a social movement becomes a task not primarily of understanding beliefs and attitudes, but rather of understanding how the organization functions.[4]

In the process of focusing on the organizational dimensions of movements, Resource Mobilization scholars have mostly abandoned the project of understanding movements through understanding their participants. In a sense, Resource Mobilization scholars have shown why an ideological understanding of movement participants is a poor analytical tool, but instead of providing a better way to understand these participants, they have essentially abandoned them. When these scholars discuss movement participants, it is under the guise of showing that their participation in a movement is not the result of an irrational ideological commitment, but rather a rational calculation aimed at securing material interests. In other words, participation in a movement is considered the result of rational calculation made by participants about what their interests are and how participation in the movement can help them secure those interests. Such an approach to understanding why people join a movement is premised on an idea that the goals of a movement are organized around interests, and that what movement participants get through participation are those interests. But such an account greatly limits an understanding of what a movement is and the great many things that participants get out of participation.

In their critique of Resource Mobilization theory's emphasis on organizational dynamics and rational action, New Social Movement theorists have argued for the need to return to focusing on the identity of the participants. They have emphasized the role that identity plays—both the personal identity of participants as well as the collective identity of the movement—in explaining participation in movements. In part this means considering a movement not simply in terms of the material rewards it may offer participants, but also its symbolic dimensions; participation is not simply about struggles over material interests, it is about struggles over symbolic values. However, New Social Movement scholars have either provided a vague notion of what identity is or fallen back into the older mode of focusing on beliefs.[5]

Scholars from the 1950s, Resource Mobilization scholars, and scholars of New Social Movements have all provided only a limited portrait of political behavior. On the one hand, scholars in the 1950s often considered social movements as instances of crowd behavior and mass rioting, where a kind of mob rule mentality pervaded and participants were likely to undertake irrational acts such as vandalism and violence. On the other hand, Resource Mobilization scholars have attempted to reclaim the rationality of the participants, but they have done so by focusing on the organization and given a portrait of political behavior as the domain of movement leaders and organizers. Scholars of the New Social Movements talk about "identity politics" as a key feature of contemporary politics, but they reduce such politics to the realm of opinions and attitudes.

While none of these bodies of scholarship offers a comprehensive theory of political behavior, each contains valuable insights about social movements. One of the many contributions of Resource Mobilization scholars has been to both show and overcome some of the limitations of an analysis of social movement participation that privileges understanding beliefs and attitudes. Building off of the insights of Resource Mobilization scholars, I also argue that beliefs and attitudes are not enough to explain participation in the Minutemen. My aim is not to deny the importance of beliefs; rather, I consider them necessary but not sufficient explanations. However, while the answer of Resource Mobilization scholars to the shortcomings of ideology is to turn to networks and organizational efforts, my answer is to turn to practices. This interest in practices is in line with the interest that New Social Movement scholarship takes in identity. I hope to build on and enrich the understanding of identity in recent scholarship through my investigation of how identity is constituted through practice.

Thinking about identity through the lens of practices is insightful because it allows us to see identity not simply as a passive state but as an active one, connected to the various things people do and seek to do to affirm who they are and want to be.[6] While this framework has usually been applied to gender and racial identities, it also opens up a richer understanding of political identities.

We can begin to think of citizenship, for example, as much more than a formal legal identity, constituted by a set of documents such as visas or passports, and consider the sets of things that people do, such as patrolling the United States / Mexico border, in constituting themselves as citizens.

In studying practices I am therefore centrally concerned with how participants behave during their involvement in a social movement. In a sense what social movement scholarship has given us are portraits of the before of movements (opinions of participants) or the after of movements (success or failure, understood in terms of securing material interests), but little in the way of the *during* of the movement. In this book, my focus is on the during of the movement. And a focus on the during means a focus on the doing.

With regard to the Minutemen, a focus on the doing means a focus on the patrols. As a result, the majority of the book takes place in the Minutemen camp or on the patrol line.

Although the Minutemen are a national organization with patrols taking place in four border states—Arizona, California, New Mexico, and Texas—the Minutemen camp I focused on was located in southern Arizona. I chose southern Arizona because it functioned as the national headquarters of the organization and tended to draw the greatest number of volunteers. Beyond this, I traveled to various locations across the United States where organizational meetings and protests took place. Overall I participated in six separate monthlong musters, in which Minutemen volunteers gather biannually to patrol the border, and attended four other weekend patrols not organized as part of these monthly musters. In total I spent over three hundred hours on actual patrol with group members. Beyond participation in patrols, I slept in the campgrounds that served as operational headquarters and followed the daily routines of members.

There are two exceptions to the book's focus on the Minutemen camp. In both chapter 1, which focuses on conversations I had with the Minutemen, and chapter 3, which is based on time I spent with Gordon at his home in Ohio, I take a step back from the camp and the patrols. I believe that both these moments help illuminate what the Minutemen are doing on the border.

The first chapter is particularly different from the rest of the book. Based on interviews, it is the only chapter that does not rely on my participant observation with the members to tell their stories. In the camp as well as on drives through the desert, at restaurants, or in the privacy of their own homes, I spent hours talking to the Minutemen about their lives. These conversations followed the protocols of what sociologists call "life histories," in which I asked the volunteers a series of open-ended questions about their pasts, interfering as little as possible so that these men could determine how they wanted to tell their stories. These life histories are deeply personal, moral accounts that provide us access not to objective facts but to people's attitudes and opinions.

What, then, is the role of the first chapter and the life histories contained within it, so attuned as they are to articulating beliefs and attitudes? How does it fit into the larger structure of the book and the argument that we need to focus on practices to understand the Minutemen?

My argument is not that beliefs don't matter, but that they can take us only so far: the life histories reveal the Minutemen's grievances but not the solutions to those grievances. While the problem can be expressed in words and thoughts, the solution is rooted in action. Related to this, I show that the Minutemen go to the border not simply to follow the protocols of a political ideology, not simply to support a government policy or to express racist opinions, but to participate in a social world and engage in the practices of soldiering. These life histories show that attitudes and beliefs are not in themselves solutions for these men: the beliefs themselves do not offer the men meaning in their lives or determine their courses of action. They merely open up possible ways of engaging with the world.

In the process of narrating their lives, the Minutemen historicize themselves, locating their lives and beliefs within past experiences, events, and relationships. The historical dimension contained in the Minutemen's life stories allows us to see that what brings them to the border is not simply an ideology, timeless and static, nor even the current historical and political moment in which they live, with its economic and cultural shifts, but rather a process. Unlike responses to survey questions or statistical data, life histories reflect process. And it is to process that we must turn to understand how the Minutemen get to the border.

The more we think about the Minutemen and what they are doing on the U.S.-Mexico border just in terms of the here and now, whether that be conceived in terms of an ideology they currently hold, or the political and economic situation of 9/11 and the war on terror, or the rise in illegal immigration, the less we understand them. Certainly all these are important; they have enabled the Minutemen, and the Minutemen are responding to them. But as they reveal most poignantly in their life histories, these volunteers also come to the border to fight battles that ostensibly ended long ago.

My argument is not just that we need to look back in time to locate a formative moment or experience, but also that we need to look at the trajectory of these men's lives. While specific historical events matter to these men, to understand the Minutemen we need to make sense not of a particular event or moment, but of a life.

Michael Kimmel, in his writings on rural militia members in America, traces the emergence of the militia to the farm crisis of the 1980s.[7] Kimmel offers a convincing account of the role of the farm crisis in the formation of the group. While it is tempting to find a similar historical moment, such as 9/11, and consider the Minutemen as an outgrowth of it, I think this would be a mistake. They did not become Minutemen now only because of a new political climate or changes in their personal convictions. These men are Minutemen today neither simply as a result of ideology nor as a result of what scholars of social movements call "political opportunity structures," that is, a political climate that enables them to exist.[8] They are Minutemen today because of the lives they've lived, and because they have reached a particular moment in those lives. Becoming a Minuteman is the result neither of a set of beliefs nor of structural forces, but of a life lived, a life that gets one to a point where going to border makes sense. By understanding these men through the trajectories of their lives, I understand them as actors who are continually making and remaking their own identities. These men, at this point in their lives, create and re-create themselves on the border as Minutemen.

But while the men patrol the border, with the exception of a few they do not live at the border. And understanding their lives away from the border was an important task for me. In part the members' everyday lives get articulated through the life histories, which detail experiences of isolation and alienation back home. But I wanted to have a firsthand sense of this, so I traveled to the homes of a handful of volunteers and spent time with them following their daily routines. The final section of chapter 3 offers an account of one such moment, which is representative of the dynamics I witnessed with the other volunteers whose homes I visited.

As mentioned earlier, this book builds on a strong ethnographic tradition of understanding social worlds by focusing on practices, and it reconsiders which practices we ought to focus on when analyzing social worlds. The claim of this book is not simply that we should focus on practices to understand the Minutemen camp, but rather that we should focus on a particular set of practices, practices that may seem counterintuitive.

Ethnographers have often located key moments in the social worlds they study that are said to articulate the meaning and structure of those worlds in particularly incisive ways. The classic example of this is Clifford Geertz's analysis of Balinese society through cockfights.[9] For Geertz the cockfight is the epitome of Balinese social life, the moment of activity from which we can capture who the Balinese are. Generations of ethnographers have followed suit, searching for their own cockfights in the worlds they study.

Similarly, Erving Goffman conceives of "action" as an analytical tool through which to explore identity. Goffman argues that forms of action that involve a high degree of risk and danger, actions that are "fateful," are the most important ones to analyze because they allow the individual to establish his or her "moral character."[10] He offers the example of gambling as one such action, mostly because of the high risk involved. That is, Goffman considers action as those activities determined by the structure of their outcomes: unknown and entailing the potential for great loss or reward. Undoubtedly the Minutemen conceive of patrolling the border as an opportunity to establish their "moral character" because of the supposed dangers that are involved, dangers that the group works hard to magnify even when they may seem minimal.

But where, really, is the action on the border? What are the activities that are most meaningful to these men's identities and on which we should focus? The commonsense approach, one used by media and scholars alike, is to assume that to understand the Minutemen, we need to focus on the moments in which they encounter illegal immigrants. These moments, after all, appear as the crux of patrolling the border, the apex of the activity.

Throughout the bulk of this book, encounters with illegal immigrants are conspicuously missing. The reason for this is that they are rarely encountered on the patrols; the encounter is *not* where the action is.

To understand the Minutemen, we need to focus not on the moment in which they encounter illegal immigrants, but on the moments in which they prepare for these encounters. My argument is that we need to focus on how they prepare for these encounters; it is there that we will find the most significant and meaningful actions these men undertake. Such an approach aligns with the larger argument of the book, which is that to understand the Minutemen, we need to focus on *how* they undertake their patrols, not, as Goffman considers with gambling, the outcomes of those patrols.

It is not until chapter 5, therefore, that we encounter illegal immigrants. In this chapter I examine a humanitarian group called the Samaritans, a group that is ostensibly radically different from the Minutemen because of what they do when they encounter illegal immigrants. But as I show, these procedures are not in fact radically different. As I hope this chapter reveals, the moment I thought would be the most important in differentiating these two groups, the moment of encounter with the object of their "politics"—the "enemy" or the "victim"—is, in a sense, the least meaningful moment. Instead, differences between the groups become apparent when one focuses on how they groups prepare for the encounters and undertake their patrols, and how the patrols fit into the lives of their members.

When we are presented with opinion surveys documenting different beliefs about issues such as immigration, we are given only a partial account of what the political consists of, of what the politics organized around immigration entails. What I hope this book shows is that ethnography offers us a chance to enrich this by studying that other dimension of political life: the one expressed not through opinions but practices; the one that leads people to patrol the border.

Notes

||||||||||||||||||||||||||||||

PREFACE

1. While the depictions of all places are real, including demographic, economic, and topographical information, unless they are publicly known the names of the places and the institutions within them have been fictionalized.

2. Doug Massey, *Backfire at the Border: Why Enforcement without Legalization Cannot Stop Illegal Immigration* (Washington, DC: Cato Institute, 2005).

3. I have thought very hard about what term to use to describe the people referred to in contemporary American discourse along a spectrum from "illegal aliens" to "undocumented migrants." My hope in using the term "illegal immigrant" is that it does not subscribe to the politics of either side. Although problematic, it is a term that neither side adopts because it lacks the political designation of their respective preferred terms. I am convinced that most of the people I write about in this book will consider my usage of illegal immigrant unsatisfactory, and that gives me comfort in the choice.

4. Compared with 1993, when 92,639 apprehensions were reported in the Tucson Sector, by 2000 the number was 616,346, accounting for over one-third of the total number of apprehensions on the southern border, by far the largest share of any of the sectors. Beyond this, according to the Department of Homeland Security, 1.7 million pounds of marijuana was seized along the border with Mexico in 2006, over a third in the Tucson Sector alone. See United States Department of Homeland Security, *Statistical Yearbook* (Washington, DC: Department of Homeland Security, 2005), table 35. See also Eric Swedlund "Drug Seizures on Border Soar," *Arizona Daily Star*, July 10, 2006.

5. United States Department of Homeland Security, Office of Immigration Studies, *Immigration Enforcement Actions, 2006*, Annual Report, May 2008.

6. United States Government Accountability Office, *Border Crossing Deaths Have Doubled since 1995*, GAO-06-770 (Washington, DC: GAO, August 2006).

7. In Greeley, for example, the Hispanic population increased from 27,502 in 1990 to 48,935 in 2000, a 77.9 percent increase. U.S. Census Bureau, *Racial and Ethnic Residential Segregation in the United States: 1980–2000*, Series CENSR-3.

8. Consider the following quote outlining the Border Patrol's redefinition of its mission: "In the wake of the terrorist attacks of September 11, 2001, the Border Patrol has experienced a tremendous change in its mission. . . . The Border Patrol has as its priority mission preventing terrorists and terrorist weapons from entering the United States. The Border Patrol will continue to advance its traditional mission by preventing illegal aliens, smugglers, narcotics, and other contraband from entering the United States as these measures directly impact the safety and security of the United States."

United States Customs and Border Protection, *National Border Patrol Strategy* (Washington, DC: Office of the Border Patrol, September 2004), 2.

9. To protect confidentiality, I use pseudonyms to identify all people unless they are public figures. Furthermore, specific biographical details that might reveal identity, but which are not consequential to the larger account, have been altered in a way that maintains their general character as best as possible.

10. Hereafter referred to simply as the Minutemen.

11. Of 193 Minutemen for whom I collected such information, 164 (85%%) were men. Of those men, 138 (84%) had served in the military in some capacity. While many had been drafted during the Vietnam War, a significant number volunteered for service, some in the Korean War but others during more recent conflicts, such as the first Gulf War. Of the people with a military background, 105 (76%) served beyond their required tour of duty, and 82 (59%) went on to have military careers or work in the military-industrial complex (including police officers, private investigators, parole officers, weapons and ammunition salespeople, and private security). Of the roughly 400 volunteers I met on the border, almost all were white. I met two African Americans and six who identified as Latino Americans.

INTRODUCTION

1. Although the group originally started as the Tombstone Militia in 2002, it was not until 2005 that it became formalized as the Minutemen, at which point a massive national mobilization campaign helped bring the large following of volunteers. Although the transition from the more localized Tombstone Militia to the Minutemen, and the dynamics of mobilization that went into it, are an important story, this book focuses on the group after its establishment as the Minutemen.

2. Mike Davis, "Vigilante Man," *Mother Jones*, May 6, 2006.

3. Joseph Farah, "Minutemen Are Heroes," *WorldNetDaily*, April 8, 2005.

4. This quote, by Rep. Kyrsten Sinema, appears on page 7 of the minutes of HB 2286, "Domestic Terrorism," State of Arizona House of Representatives, 48th legislature, 2007.

5. United States House of Representatives, "Securing Our Borders: What Have We Learned from Government Initiatives and Citizen Patrols?" Hearing before Committee on Government Reform, 109th Congress, first session, May 12, 2005, Serial no. 109-24.

6. Consider, for example, the two books that have given extensive focus to the Minutemen: Armando Navarro's *The Immigration Crisis: Nativism, Armed Vigilantism, and the Rise of a Countervailing Movement* (Lanham, MD: Altamira Press, 2009); and Roxanne Doty's *The Law into Their Own Hands: Immigration and the Politics of Exceptionalism* (Tucson: University of Arizona Press, 2009). Both authors use the category of "right-wing" to define the Minutemen and position them as part of an "anti-immigrant movement," which, as Doty puts it, is rooted in a set of "attitudes" or "sentiments" that include "racism" and "white supremacy." "Ideologically," writes Navarro, the Minutemen "were nativistic, racist, and xenophobic, especially towards Mexicanos. They adhered to a White nationalism that was permeated by a WASP ethos. . . . They were driven by a hatred of undocumented immigrants, especially Mexicanos. . . . Their xenophobic perceptions and attitudes were based on their assertion that 'brown people' were egregiously changing the ethnic and cultural makeup of the U.S." (194).

7. Robert Stallings, "Patterns of Belief In Social Movements: Clarifications from an Analysis of Environmental Groups," *Sociological Quarterly* 14, 4 (September 1973): 465–80.

8. See, for example, Kathleen Blee and K. Cresap, "Conservative and Right-Wing Movements," *Annual Review of Sociology* 36 (2010): 269–86.

9. I am thinking here specifically of the account given by Robert Putnam in *Bowling Alone: The Collapse and Revival of American Community* (New York: Simon and Schuster, 2001), and by Richard Sennett in *Corrosion of Character: The Personal Consequences of Work in the New Capitalism* (New York: Norton, 2000).

10. Seymour Martin Lipset, "Democracy and Working-Class Authoritarianism," *American Sociological Review* 24 (1959): 490.

11. Alexis de Tocqueville, *Democracy in America* (New York: Library of America, [1835] 2004).

12. These remarks came following a meeting between President Bush and the Homeland Security Council, October 29, 2001. The full transcript is available at John T. Woolley and Gerhard Peters's American Presidency Project, University of California, Santa Barbara. http://www.presidency.ucsb.edu/ws/index.php?pid=63772&st=&st1=.

13. Chris Simcox, "Enough Is Enough!" *Tombstone Tumbleweed* 16, 17, October 24, 2002.

14. See Blee and Cresap, "Conservative and Right-Wing Movements."

CHAPTER 1

1. See, for example, Wendy Bracewell, "Rape in Kosovo: Masculinity and Serbian Nationalism," *Nations and Nationalism* 6, 4 (2000): 563–90; Cynthia Enloe, *Bananas, Beaches, and Bases: Making Feminist Sense of International Politics* (Los Angeles: University of California Press, 1990); Lesley Gill, "Creating Citizens, Making Men: The Military and Masculinity in Bolivia," *Cultural Anthropology* 12, 4 (1997): 527–50; Genevive Lloyd, "Selfhood, War and Masculinity," in *Feminist Challenges: Social and Political Theory*, ed. C. Pateman and E. Gross (Boston: Northeastern University Press, 1986); D.H.J. Morgan, "Theatre of War: Combat, the Military and Masculinities," in *Theorizing Masculinities*, ed. H. Brod and M. Kaufman (London: Sage, 1994); George Mosse, *The Image of Man: The Creation of Modern Masculinity* (New York: Oxford University Press, 1996); Joanne Nagel. "Masculinity and Nationalism: Gender and Sexuality in the Making of Nations," *Ethnic and Racial Studies* 21, 2 (1998): 242–69; J. M. Oca, "'As Our Muscles Get Softer Our Missile Race Becomes Stronger': Cultural Citizenship and the 'Muscle Gap,'" *Journal of Historical Sociology* 18, 3 (2005): 145–72; C. R. Snyder, *Citizen-Soldier and Manly Warriors: Military Service and Gender in the Civic Republic Tradition* (Lanham, MD: Rowman & Littlefield, 1999); and Nira Yuval-Davis, *Gender and Nation* (London: Sage, 1998).

2. Nagel, "Masculinity and Nationalism," 248, 252.

CHAPTER 2

1. Although Camp Vigilance is technically the name of the Minutemen camp in California, I use it here to refer to the Arizona camp.

2. Jurgen Harbermas, *The Structural Transformation of the Public Sphere: An Inquiry Into a Category of Bourgeois Society* (Boston: MIT Press, [1962] 1989).

3. Nina Eliasoph, *Avoiding Politics: How Americans Produce Apathy in Everyday Life* (Boston: Cambridge University Press, 1989).

4. Daniel Dayan and Elihu Katz, *Media Events: The Live Broadcasting of History* (Cambridge: Cambridge University Press, 1992).

5. Erving Goffman, *Asylums: Essays on the Social Situation of Mental Patients and Other Inmates* (New York: Doubleday, 1961).

6. Ibid., 15.

7. Ibid., 22.

8. Nagel, "Masculinity and Nationalism," 243.

9. Yuval-Davis, *Gender and Nation*.

10. See, for example, Jessica Conway, "Reversion Back to a State of Nature in the United States Southern Borderlands: A Look at the Potential Causes of Action to Curb Vigilante Activity on The United States / Mexico Border," *Mercer Law Review* 56 (2005): 1419–25.

11. Thomas Gieryn, "Boundary-Work and the Demarcation of Science from Nonscience: Strains and Interests in Professional Interests of Scientists," *American Sociological Review* 48 (1983): 781–95.

12. "Securing Our Border: What Have We learned from Government Initiatives and Citizen Patrols?" Hearing before the Committee on Government Reform, House of Representatives, 109th Congress, first session, May 12, 2005, Serial no. 109-24.

13. On criticisms of Putnam's data, see for example: Claude Fischer, "Ever-More Rooted Americans," *City & Community* 1,2 (2002): 177–98. Nicholas Lemann, "Kicking In Groups," *The Atlantic Online*, April 1996. Pamela Paxton, "Is Social Capital Declining in the United States? A Multiple Indicator Assessment," *American Journal of Sociology* 105, 1 (1999): 88–127.

CHAPTER 3

1. Pierre Bourdieu, *The Logic of Practice* (Stanford: Stanford University Press, 1990).

2. Goffman, *Asylums*.

3. John Van Mannen, "Boundary Crossings: Major Strategies of Organizational Socialization," in *Career Issues in Human Resource Management*, ed. R. Katz (Englewood Cliffs, NJ: Prentice-Hall, 1982), 101.

4. U.S. Census Bureau, *State and County QuickFacts; 2010 Census Redistricting Data* (Public Law 94-171), Summary File, 2010, tables P1, P2, P3, P4, H1.

CHAPTER 4

1. It is worth noting that Roger did not end up taking Tom to the hospital the next day. In large part this was because of Tom's insistence that he could "tough it out." The incident serves as another example of how these men sought to define themselves as "masculine" through suffering.

2. It is possible that I am wrong, but from knowing Jack, my belief is that he wanted me to write the story he was telling me. In fact, I think that by saying that he did not want me to write about it, he was strategically dramatizing the story and trying to induce me to pay attention and write about it. That said, if I thought that publishing the story he told me would somehow have negative consequences for him, I would not have included it.

3. Mary Douglas, *Purity and Danger* (London: Routledge, 1966).

4. I thank Shehzad Nadeem for these insights.

5. Clifford Geertz, "Thick Description: Toward an Interpretative Theory of Culture," in *The Interpretation of Cultures: Selected Essays* (New York: Basic Books, 1973).

6. Victor Turner, *Dramas, Fields, and Metaphors: Symbolic Action in Human Society* (Ithaca: Cornell University Press, 1975).

7. This interpretation follows that offered by William Gibson in *Warrior Dreams: Paramilitary Culture in Post-Vietnam America* (New York: Hill and Wang, 1994). Focusing on paramilitary culture after Vietnam, Gibson says, "It is hardly surprising, then, that American men—lacking confidence in the government and the economy, troubled by the changing relations between the sexes, uncertain of their identity or their future— began to dream, to fantasize about the powers and features of another kind of man who could retake and reorder the world. And the hero of all these dreams was the paramilitary warrior" (11).

8. Leon Festinger, Henry W. Reicken, and Stanley Schachter, *When Prophecy Fails: A Social and Psychological Study of a Modern Group That Predicted the Destruction of the World* (Minneapolis: University of Minnesota Press, 1956).

CHAPTER 5

1. The other two are Humane Borders and No More Deaths.

2. Based on data for forty-three meetings I attended, the average number of attendees was twenty-three, of whom sixteen were women and seven were men.

CONCLUSION

1. Superior Court of the State of California, County of Los Angeles, "Supplemental Declaration of Kim Dunbar in Support of Order to Show Cause for Child Custody and Visitation," October 29, 2001, Case no. BD 079 044, 4.

2. Ibid., "Attachment to Order to Show Cause," 1.

3. Ibid., 5.

4. In 1999 Roger Barnett, who owned a 22,000-acre ranch in southern Arizona, established an organization known as Concerned Citizens of Cochise County (CCCC). The thirty or so local ranchers who were members of the group were upset that their property was continuously being trespassed on, and they started to patrol each other's land in an effort that they described as "protecting our rights." Along with CCCC, a second organization emerged in mid-2000, calling themselves Ranch Rescue. In a press release announcing the formation of the group, founder Jack Foote said he was recruiting people to "help ranchers on the Arizona / Mexico border cope with the damage to their property caused by thousands of criminal trespassers."

By October 2000 officer safety bulletins from the U.S. Department of Justice were alerting local sheriffs to be wary of ranchers patrolling the border, although the county sheriff was sympathetic to the ranchers' cause: "People have been pushed to the point of desperation and exasperation, of feeling that they have to take the situation under control themselves because the government's not going to do it for them." The sheriff's sympathies notwithstanding, an attack on two illegal immigrants from El Salvador on March 20, 2003, led to the arrest of two group members. Along with a prison sentence in the criminal trial for two members, five of the members involved suffered enormous financial losses in a civil trial that followed.

5. Stuart Emmrich et al., "31 Places to Go This Summer," *New York Times*, June 1, 2008.

APPENDIX

1. Steven Buechler, "New Social Movement Theories," *Sociological Quarterly* 36, 3 (1995): 441–64. See also Steven Buechler, *Social Movements in Advanced Capitalism: The Political Economy and Cultural Construction of Social Activism* (New York: Oxford University Press, 1999); E. Larana, H. Johnson, and J. Gusfield, eds., *New Social Movements: From Ideology to Identity* (Philadelphia: Temple University Press, 1994); Alberto Melucci, "The New Social Movements: A Theoretical Approach," *Social Science Information* 19 (1980): 199–226; Alberto Melucci, "Getting Involved: Identity and Mobilization in Social Movements," *Research in Social Movements, Conflicts and Change* 1 (1988): 329–48; Nelson Pichardo, "New Social Movements: A Critical Review," *Annual Review of Sociology* 23 (1997): 411–30.

2. John McCarthy and Mayer Zald provide a concise account of this approach, in which a social movement is defined as "a set of opinions and beliefs in a population which represents preferences for changing some elements of the social structure and/or reward distribution of a society." "Resource Mobilization and Social Movements: A Partial Theory," *American Journal of Sociology* 82, 6 (1977): 1217.

3. See, for example, Doug McAdam, *Political Process and the Development of Black Insurgency, 1930–1970* (Chicago: University of Chicago Press, 1982); Craig Jenkins, "Resource Mobilization Theory and the Study of Social Movements," *Annual Review of Sociology* 9 (1983): 527–53.

4. In Resource Mobilization theory, when the individual participant is considered, the focus is not on his or her beliefs but rather on the individual's location in the social structure and on how social ties connect the individual to the organization. Methodologically, Resource Mobilization theorists replace opinion surveys with organizational and network analysis and see the connection between beliefs and movement participation as marginal. An influential example of this approach is given by Doug McAdam in his work on civil rights activists. Focusing on student activists involved in the "Freedom Summer" campaign of 1964, McAdam shows that attitudinal differences did not significantly differentiate those students who traveled to Mississippi from those who did not. But while attitudinal differences were not great, there was a significant difference in terms of organizational connections and social networks between those who did and did not participate: students who were well integrated into political organizations and who had

strong social ties to other student volunteers were more like to participate, regardless of attitudes. McAdam, *Freedom Summer* (New York: Oxford University Press, 1990).

5. One the field's prominent figures, Mario Diani, for example, says that "Only those actors, sharing the same beliefs and sense of belongingness, can be considered to be part of a social movement." Diani, "The Concept of Social Movements," *Sociological Review* 40, 1 (1992): 9.

6. Candace West and Don Zimmerman, "Doing Gender," *Gender and Society* 1, 2 (1987): 125–51.

7. Michael Kimmel and Amy Ferber, "'White Men Are This Nation': 'Right Wing' Militias and the Restoration of Rural American Masculinity," *Rural Sociology* 65, 4 (2000): 582–604.

8. Sidney Tarrow, *Power in Movement: Social Movements, Collective Action and Politics* (Boston: Cambridge University Press, 1994).

9. Clifford Geertz, "Deep Play: Notes on the Balinese Cockfight," in *The Interpretation of Cultures: Selected Essays* (New York: Basic Books, 1973).

10. Erving Goffman, "Where the Action Is," in *Interaction Ritual: Essays on Face to Face Behavior* (New York: Doubleday, 1967), 185–86.

Works Cited

||||||||||||||||||||||||||||||

Bell, D., ed. *The Radical Right*. Garden City, NY: Doubleday, (1955) 1963.

Blee, K., and K. Cresap. "Conservative and Right-Wing Movements." *Annual Review of Sociology* 36 (2010): 269–86.

Bourdieu, P. *The Logic of Practice*. Stanford: Stanford University Press, 1990.

Bracewell, W. "Rape in Kosovo: Masculinity and Serbian Nationalism." *Nations and Nationalism* 6, 4 (2000): 563–90.

Buechler, S. "New Social Movement Theories." *Sociological Quarterly* 36, 3 (1995): 441–64.

———. *Social Movements in Advanced Capitalism: The Political Economy and Cultural Construction of Social Activism*. New York: Oxford University Press, 1999.

Conway, J. "Reversion Back to a State of Nature in the United States Southern Borderlands: A Look at the Potential Causes of Action to Curb Vigilante Activity on the United States / Mexico Border." *Mercer Law Review* 56 (2005): 1419–25.

Davis, M. "Vigilante Man." *Mother Jones*. May 6, 2006.

Dayan, D., and E. Katz. *Media Events: The Live Broadcasting of History*. Cambridge: Cambridge University Press, 1992.

Diani, M. "The Concept of Social Movements." *Sociological Review* 40, 1 (1992): 1–25.

Doty, R. *The Law into Their Own Hands: Immigration and the Politics of Exceptionalism*. Tucson: University of Arizona Press, 2009.

Douglas, M. *Purity and Danger: An Analysis of the Concepts of Pollution and Taboo*. London: Routledge, (1966) 2002.

Eliasoph, N. *Avoiding Politics: How Americans Produce Apathy in Everyday Life*. New York: Cambridge University Press, 1989.

Emmrich, S., et al. "31 Places to Go This Summer." *New York Times*. June 1, 2008.

Enloe, C. *Bananas, Beaches, and Bases: Making Feminist Sense of International Politics*. Los Angeles: University of California Press, 1990.

Farah, J. "Minutemen Are Heroes." *WorldNetDaily*. April 8, 2005.

Festinger, L., H. W. Riecken, and S. Schachter. *When Prophecy Fails: A Social and Psychological Study of a Modern Group That Predicted the Destruction of the World*. Minneapolis: University of Minnesota Press, 1956.

Fischer, C. "Ever-More Rooted Americans," *City & Community* 1, 2 (2002): 77–98.

Geertz, C. "Deep Play: Notes on the Balinese Cockfight." In *The Interpretation of Cultures: Selected Essays*. New York: Basic Books, 1973.

———. "'From the Native's Point of View': On the Nature of Anthropological Knowledge." In *Local Knowledge: Further Essays in Interpretive Anthropology*. New York: Basic Books, 1983.

———. "Thick Description: Toward an Interpretative Theory of Culture." In *The Interpretation of Cultures: Selected Essays*. New York: Basic Books, 1973.

Gibson, J. W. *Warrior Dreams: Paramilitary Culture in Post-Vietnam America*. New York: Hill and Wang, 1994.

Gieryn, T. "Boundary-Work and the Demarcation of Science from Non-science: Strains and Interests in Professional Interests of Scientists." *American Sociological Review* 48 (1983): 781–95.

Gill, L. "Creating Citizens, Making Men: The Military and Masculinity in Bolivia." *Cultural Anthropology* 12, 4 (1997): 527–50.

Ginsberg, A. "America." In *Howl and Other Poems*. New York: City Lights Books, 1956.

Goffman, E. *Asylums: Essays on the Social Situation of Mental Patients and Other Inmates*. New York: Doubleday, 1961.

———. "Where the Action Is." In *Interaction Ritual: Essays on Face to Face Behavior*. New York: Doubleday, 1967.

Habermas, J. *The Structural Transformation of the Public Sphere: An Inquiry into a Category of Bourgeois Society*. Boston: MIT Press, (1962) 1989.

Jenkins, C. "Resource Mobilization Theory and the Study of Social Movements." *Annual Review of Sociology* 9 (1983): 527–53.

Kaufman, S. *The Ageless Self: Sources of Meaning in Late Life*. Madison: University of Wisconsin Press, 1994.

Kimmel, M., and A. Ferber. "'White Men Are This Nation': 'Right Wing' Militias and the Restoration of Rural American Masculinity." *Rural Sociology* 65, 4 (2000): 582–604.

Larana, E., H. Johnson, and J. Gusfield, eds. *New Social Movements: From Ideology to Identity*. Philadelphia: Temple University Press, 1994.

Lemann, N. "Kicking in Groups," *The Atlantic Online*, April 1996.

Lipset, S. M. "Democracy and Working-Class Authoritarianism." *American Sociological Review* 24 (1959):482–501.

Lloyd, G. "Selfhood, War and Masculinity." In *Feminist Challenges: Social and Political Theory*. Edited by C. Pateman and E. Gross. Boston: Northeastern University Press, 1986.

Massey, D. *Backfire at the Border: Why Enforcement without Legalization Cannot Stop Illegal Immigration*. Washington, DC: Cato Institute, 2005.

McAdam, D. *Freedom Summer*. New York: Oxford University Press, 1990.

———. *Political Process and the Development of Black Insurgency, 1930–1970*. Chicago: University of Chicago Press, 1982.

McCarthy, J., and M. Zald. "Resource Mobilization and Social Movements: A Partial Theory." *American Journal of Sociology* 82, 6 (1997): 1212–41.

Melucci, A. "Getting Involved: Identity and Mobilization in Social Movements." *Research in Social Movements, Conflicts and Change* 1 (1988): 329–48.

———. "The New Social Movements: A Theoretical Approach." *Social Science Information* 19 (1980): 199–226.

Morgan, D.H.J. "Theatre of War: Combat, the Military and Masculinities." In *Theorizing Masculinities*. Edited by H. Brod and M. Kaufman. London: Sage, 1994.

Mosse, G. *The Image of Man: The Creation of Modern Masculinity*. New York: Oxford University Press, 1996.

Nagel, J. "Masculinity and Nationalism: Gender and Sexuality in the Making of Nations." *Ethnic and Racial Studies* 21, 2 (1998): 242–69.

Navarro, A. *The Immigration Crisis: Nativism, Armed Vigilantism, and the Rise of a Countervailing Movement*. Lanham, MD: Altamira Press, 2009.

Oca, J. M. "'As Our Muscles Get Softer Our Missile Race Becomes Stronger': Cultural Citizenship and the 'Muscle Gap.'" *Journal of Historical Sociology* 18, 3 (2005): 145–72.

Paxton, P. "Is Social Capital Declining in the United States? A Multiple Indicator Assessment," *American Journal of Sociology* 105, 1 (1999): 88–127.

Pichardo, N. "New Social Movements: A Critical Review." *Annual Review of Sociology* 23 (1997): 411–30.

Putnam, R. *Bowling Alone: The Collapse and Revival of American Community*. New York: Simon and Schuster, 2001.

Sennett, R. *Corrosion of Character: The Personal Consequences of Work in the New Capitalism*. New York: Norton, 2000.

Simcox, C. "Enough Is Enough!" *Tombstone Tumbleweed* 16, 17. October 24, 2002.

Snyder, C. R. *Citizen-Soldier and Manly Warriors: Military Service and Gender in the Civic Republic Tradition*. Lanham, MD: Rowman & Littlefield, 1999.

Stallings, R. "Patterns of Belief In Social Movements: Clarifications from an Analysis of Environmental Groups." *Sociological Quarterly* 14, 4 (September 1973): 465–80.

Swedlund, E. "Drug Seizures on Border Soar." *Arizona Daily Star*. July 10, 2006.

Tarrow, S. *Power in Movement: Social Movements, Collective Action and Politics*. New York: Cambridge University Press, 1994.

Tocqueville, A. de. *Democracy in America*. New York: Library of America, (1835) 2004.

Turner, V. *Dramas, Fields, and Metaphors: Symbolic Action in Human Society*. Ithaca: Cornell University Press, 1975.

United States Census Bureau. *Racial and Ethnic Residential Segregation in the United States: 1980–2000*. Series CENSR-3.

———. *State and County QuickFacts; 2010 Census Redistricting Data* (Public Law 94-171). Summary File, 2010, tables P1, P2, P3, P4, H1.

United States Customs and Border Protection. *National Border Patrol Strategy*. Washington, DC: Office of the Border Patrol, September 2004.

United States Department of Homeland Security. *Statistical Yearbook*. Washington, DC: Department of Homeland Security, 2005, table 35..

———. Office of Immigration Studies. *Immigration Enforcement Actions, 2006*. Annual Report. May 2008.

United States Government Accountability Office. *Border Crossing Deaths Have Doubled since 1995*. GAO-06-770. Washington, DC: GAO, August 2006.

United States House of Representatives. "Securing Our Borders: What Have We Learned from Government Initiatives and Citizen Patrols?" Hearing before Committee on Government Reform, 109th Congress, first session, May 12, 2005. Serial no. 109-24.

Van Mannen, J. "Boundary Crossings: Major Strategies of Organizational Socialization." In *Career Issues in Human Resource Management*. Edited by R. Katz. Englewood Cliffs, NJ: Prentice-Hall, 1982.

West, C., and D. Zimmerman. "Doing Gender." *Gender and Society* 1, 2 (1987): 125–51.

Yuval-Davis, N. *Gender and Nation*. London: Sage, 1998.

Zald, Mayer. "Ideologically Structured Action: An Enlarged Agenda for Social Movement Research." *Mobilization* 5, 1 (2000): 1–16.

Index

||||||||||||||||||||||||||||||||